MEET THE BRETHREN

AUTHORS

Robert G. Clouse   Professor of History
Indiana State University, Terre Haute, IN

Donald F. Durnbaugh   Professor of Church History
Bethany Theological Seminary, Oak Brook, IL

David B. Eller   Professor of History
Bluffton College, Bluffton, OH

Jerry R. Flora   Professor of New Testament and Theology
Ashland Theological Seminary, Ashland, OH

Marcus Miller   Physician
Covington, OH

Nedra A. Pike   Nurse
Toledo, OH

Howard J. Surbey   Deceased
Littletown, PA

BOARD OF DIRECTORS
THE BRETHREN ENCYCLOPEDIA, INC.

MEET THE BRETHREN

Edited by

Donald F. Durnbaugh

Elgin, IL: The Brethren Press for The Brethren Encyclopedia, Inc., 1984

Those providing photographs used in the portfolio of illustrations are acknowledged in the photo captions. Special appreciation is due the Brethren Historical Library and Archives (BHLA), Elgin, IL, which was the source of many of the photographs.

ISBN 0-87178-559-5

TABLE OF CONTENTS

Preface   7

Brethren, 1708-1883
      Donald F. Durnbaugh   9

Old German Baptist Brethren
      Marcus Miller 29

Brethren Church
      Jerry R. Flora 41

Illustrations 53

Church of the Brethren
      David B. Eller 69

Dunkard Brethren
      Howard J. Surbey/Nedra A. Pike 93

Fellowship of Grace Brethren Churches
      Robert G. Clouse 101

Additional Reading 115

Topical Index 117

PREFACE

Since the origin of the Brethren movement in Germany in 1708, several distinct denominations have emerged from it with varied doctrinal emphases. A three-way division in 1881-1883 resulted in the formation of the Old German Baptist Brethren, the German Baptist Brethren (known since 1908 as the Church of the Brethren), and the Brethren Church. The last-named body experienced division in 1939 with the orgainzation of the National Fellowship of Brethren Churches (known since 1976 as the Fellowship of Grace Brethren Churches). In 1926 the Dunkard Brethren were formed as a division of the Church of the Brethren.

Representatives of these Brethren denominations have worked together since 1977 to produce a reference work called *The Brethren Encyclopedia*. Its intent is to provide thorough and dependable coverage of "Brethren life, belief, practice, and heritage." The encyclopedia was developed by an editorial staff working at Oak Brook, Illinois; a financial and promotional office was located at the Germantown "mother church" in Philadelphia, Pennsylvania. The first two volumes, which contain about six thousand articles, were completed in late 1983 and distributed in March, 1984. The third volume, which contains extensive lists of ministers and missionaries, maps, statistics, and a bibliography, is scheduled for release in late 1984.

The Board of Directors of the encyclopedia decided in August, 1983, to publish a small book describing the five major Brethren bodies, based on articles included in *The Brethren Encyclopedia*. An article covering the common history from 1708 to 1883 provides an introduction to the denominational articles. Asterisks appearing in these articles refer to cross-referenced articles in the parent encyclopedia. An accompanying portfolio of photographs was selected from the 510 illustrations incorporated into the encyclopedia. D. F. Durnbaugh, Charles W. Turner, and Dale V. Ulrich were named as the publication committee for this book.

The book has two purposes: it enables readers belonging to one of the five participating Brethren groups to inform themselves quickly about the history and beliefs of the other Brethren; it also enables non-Brethren readers to obtain in brief compass authoritative information about the Brethren family of Christians. Those who issue the book trust that it will be used, in the motto of the Germantown printer Christopher Sauer, "for the glory of God and our neighbor's good."

D. F. Durnbaugh

Brethren, 1708-1883. The Brethren movement began in Aug., 1708, in an obscure German principality, *Sayn-Wittgenstein-Hohenstein. Five men and three women, most under thirty years of age, took there a solemn covenant of "good conscience with God, to take up all the commandments of Jesus Christ as an easy yoke, and thus to follow the Lord Jesus . . . even unto a blessed end." Primarily of *Reformed Church background, the eight individuals had been influenced by the radical wing of *pietist renewal (*Radical German Pietism). The outcome of their religious quest was expulsion by the state from their homes in several German states, *France, and *Switzerland. They sought and found refuge in Wittgenstein after 1700. As they there studied the Scriptures, read church history, and discussed doctrines, they came to agreement on a view of the *church consonant with that developed by the 16th-century *Anabaptists, with whose descendants, the *Mennonites, they had close contact. Thus the Brethren were formed at the confluence of basic Protestant faith, pietist reform, and anabaptist ecclesiology.

Many of those who became Brethren had been converted or "awakened" by the itinerant minister *E. C. Hochmann von Hochenau, a Radical Pietist. Before those gathered at Wittgenstein sent an invitation in early summer, 1708, to fellow Pietists in the *Palatinate to join in their proposed baptism and church covenant, they wrote to Hochmann asking his view of the biblical form of *baptism. Hochmann replied that *infant baptism had no biblical warrant, and that believer's baptism was fitting, but also that such action dare not be made a sectarian matter. The first eight at Schwarzenau went ahead with their plan to baptize and to form a community, believing they had their mentor's approval. He was later to criticize their practices as unduly restrictive.

FORMATION AND EXPANSION. The first Brethren baptism took place in the *Eder River near *Schwarzenau. The exact site and date (early Aug., 1708) were kept secret, as was the name of the man (chosen by lot) who baptized *Alexander Mack, Sr., their leader and first minister. Mack baptized his baptizer and the remaining six — *Anna Margaretha Mack, *Andreas Boni, *Johanna Nöthiger Boni, *Johann Kipping, *Johanna Kipping, *Georg Grebe, and *Lukas Vetter. They did not wish their community to be called after any individual; in fact, they chose no name at all, referring to themselves simply as "brethren." Since baptism of adults was considered rebaptism (they had all received Reformed or *Lutheran baptism as infants) and was illegal under the laws of the Holy Roman Empire, some concern for their security may have been present as well. Indeed, when rulers of surrounding territories heard of the event they registered immediate protest with Wittgenstein's sovereign, Count *Henrich Albrecht. He, however, was of pietist inclination himself and defended the recent settlers. The neighboring rulers then denounced the new religious dissenters to the imperial authorities. The latter proceeded so slowly that inquiry was not completed until 1720, after the Brethren left the area.

Although little is known in detail about the young congregation in Schwarzenau, it is clear that early members generated great evangelistic fervor. Large meetings were held in Schwarzenau and surrounding villages. So many attended meetings in Schwarzenau that these were often held outdoors on a lawn still known as the "Anabaptist yard." Brethren sent out evangelists to make converts in other parts of Germany, Switzerland, and the *Netherlands.

A large branch congregation was founded in *Ysenburg-Büdingen-Marienborn, northeast of Frankfurt/-Main. As in Wittgenstein, considerable freedom of religion obtained there, attracting religious separatists driven from their homes elsewhere. A series of baptisms (1711-15) conducted by Mack and others won converts among the Marienborn settlers. When Brethren began to bring subjects of Marienborn into their fold as well as the settlers, local authorities forbade such activity under penalty of expulsion. The only extant letter of Mack was written in 1711 to plead for a stay of expulsion imposed on a widow and a daughter baptized by Mack.

Unwilling to give up their faith, the Marienborn Brethren left in 1715 and found asylum in the town of *Krefeld on the lower *Rhine River. Mennonites enjoyed toleration there because of their economic contribution to the textile industry. Brethren were so similar to the Mennonites in belief and practice that they were considered just another variant of Mennonites. However, whereas the Mennonites were content to perpetuate their belief within their own families, the aggressive Brethren reached out to convert not only the host Mennonites but also members of the *established churches, inviting repression. About 1716 Brethren ministers baptized in the Wupper River six men of the Reformed confession from Solingen. These *Solingen Brethren were arrested and sentenced to life imprisonment at hard labor at *Jülich for refusing to conform to one of the three established faiths. They were freed through the efforts of Dutch citizens after nearly four years of harsh incarceration.

Brethren activity extended to northern Germany (*Altona near Hamburg), to the Palatinate (*Eppstein), and to Switzerland (Bern and Basel). The leader *Christian Liebe was seized in Bern in 1714 and condemned, along with *Bernese Anabaptists, as a *galley slave in Italy. He was freed from this draconian punishment in 1716.

Brethren considered criticism coming from other religious groups to be as troublesome as pressure from the state. The first Brethren publication was in response to a series of critical questions from *E. L. Gruber, a Radical Pietist who later became the leader of the rival *Community of True Inspiration. This was the tract *Grundforschende Fragen (Basic Questions), published in 1713. Two years later Alexander Mack, Sr., wrote a doctrinal treatise, *Rechte und Ordnungen (Rights and Ordinances), which presented the Brethren position on controversial issues, using the format of a dialogue between father and son. Possibly the last Brethren publication in Europe was the *hymnal, *Geistreiches Gesang-Buch (Spiritual Songbook) of 1720, which contained one hundred Brethren-authored hymn texts among a selection of other *hymns.

RELOCATION IN NORTH AMERICA. Despite Brethren expansion elsewhere, the largest Brethren congregation remained the original one at Schwarzenau. When a coregent, Count *August, took office in Wittgenstein in 1719, intense pressure was placed upon the Brethren. This, added to the recurrent economic problems of the area and increased competition from other religious groups, led to the Brethren decision to relocate. In 1720 forty Brethren families moved to Surhuisterveen in West Friesland aided by funds from Dutch *Collegiants. They remained there until 1729, when almost all of the group emigrated to North America. Those remaining tended to join the Mennonites or drift into individualistic religious separatism.

The Mack-led group was not the first to leave Europe. Some twenty families from the Krefeld congregation had left for *Pennsylvania in 1719, in part because of internal dissension. Most settled in *Germantown, north of Philadelphia, a village founded in 1683 by Mennonites/Quakers from Krefeld. Other Brethren settled inland in areas known as *Skippack, Oley, *Falckner's Swamp, and *Conestoga. The dispersion made it difficult for the newcomers to reorganize as a congregation. It was not until Christmas Day, 1723, that *Peter Becker, chosen as their leader, officiated at the first Brethren *baptisms and *love feast in the New World. The "first fruits" were former Mennonites living along the Schuylkill River.

According to a later chronicler the baptisms began as such a powerful revival that "the whole region was moved thereby." In the fall of 1724 all fourteen male members at Germantown embarked on an evangelistic journey into the hinterlands, calling on those formerly in the fellowship and those known as religious dissenters. The first area visited, around Indian Creek (*Harleysville, PA), did not receive a separate organization because adherents there were considered to belong to the Germantown congregation. Coventry, near what later became Pottstown, was the second congregation formed in colonial America, followed by *Conestoga in what became Lancaster Co. Other congregations followed, including one at Amwell, NJ, led by the well-known figure *Johannes Naas.

The Conestoga congregation had a troubled development. The leader there was *J. Conrad Beissel, an able but imperious figure. Beissel's confidence in the divine inspiration of his own ideas and innovations (*sabbatarianism, *celibacy, etc.) soon led to tension with and then *schism from the main Brethren movement. In 1728 he "gave back" his baptism to the Brethren and later moved farther west to live as a hermit. Others followed, leading to the origin of the *Ephrata Community in 1732 with Beissel as "superintendent." This first Protestant monastic institution in America was noted for its cultural achievements—art, manuscript illumination (*Fraktur), choral music, printing—and attracted many Brethren to its fold. Although the compilers of the community's chronicle, the *Chronicon Ephratense (1786), were at pains to show Beissel's independent genius, it contains valuable information about the early Brethren.

Thus it was that when Alexander Mack, Sr., arrived in Pennsylvania in 1729 with a colony from West Friesland he found a divided fellowship. His best efforts to repair the breach failed, owing in large part to Beissel's intransigence. After Mack's death in 1735 and a religious awakening among younger members, there was a large-scale exodus of Brethren from Germantown to Ephrata which included Mack's own son, *Alexander Mack, Jr. He, however, returned in 1748 to Germantown, where he became an outstanding leader, noted for his literary gifts, letter writing, and a warm spirit.

Brethren expansion along the Atlantic seaboard was substantial but not numerically impressive. By 1770 a careful census compiled by *Morgan Edwards, a Baptist pastor, enumerated fifteen congregations in Pennsylvania, one in *New Jersey, five in *Maryland, one in *Virginia, and six in *North and *South Carolina. Edwards counted more than 1,500 baptized members and 42 ministers. He estimated the number of individuals related to the Brethren at nearly five times the adult membership. More recent and detailed scholarship indicates that Edwards' figures were not complete, with several additional settlements of Brethren, for example, identifiable in the Carolinas. No accurate total is available.

Brethren numerical growth was noticed and criticized by Reformed and Lutheran clergy in colonial America, for converts often came from their parishes. Reports of these clergymen to ecclesiastical superiors in Europe noted with disapproval and dismay the numbers of those who had "gone over to the Tunkers." Many Mennonites and the related *Amish found their way to the Brethren, attracted by the similar view of the church, similar practices, and the greater fervor of the Brethren.

SETTLEMENT AND DEVELOPMENT. The Brethren pattern of settlement in America followed that created by earlier German immigrants. Most arrived in Philadelphia, sought cheap land for farming, and built substantial barns and modest homes. They lived quiet and productive lives. When their numerous offspring needed land for farms of their own, additional territory was located along the Monocacy Road in Maryland, then farther south in the *Shenandoah Valley of Virginia, and on into the Carolinas. Brethren avoided those regions where *slavery was prevalent.

Although Brethren development was largely rural, a few urban centers were included. Germantown, home of the mother congregation in the USA, was absorbed by Philadelphia. A daughter congregation in Philadelphia (1817ff.) was led by *Peter Keyser, Jr., active in city affairs. The *language shift from German to English took place first in the Philadelphia area. This was marked by the publication in 1791 of the first Brethren hymnal in English, *The Christian's Duty. Another urban congregation was founded in Baltimore during the late 18th century, with *Samuel Sauer the leading figure. Neither the Philadelphia nor the Baltimore congregations flourished in the 19th century, and Baltimore was actually disbanded. Generally, urban populations were not receptive to Brethren values.

Brethren tended to settle near other members, forming enclaves. Soon after a settlement was established, meetings for religious service began in their homes. When leaders of older congregations reached them a congregation was organized and resident church officers were chosen from their ranks in the *free ministry pattern. Because church buildings, elaborate organization, and salaried leadership were not essential in the Brethren understanding of the Christian faith, this form of congregational life was well adapted to the *frontier situation. It was not until 1770 that the first Brethren *meetinghouse was constructed in Germantown. In 1980 it was still standing, although in altered and expanded form. The oldest unchanged meetinghouse, Pricetown, stands in 1980 near Reading, PA.

In the 19th century, Brethren began to build simply
styled wooden structures to accommodate the large
numbers of Brethren who gathered for the annual love
feasts. These assemblies overflowed the private homes
where meetings ordinarily were held, although houses
were often constructed with sliding or swinging wall parti-
tions to accept larger meetings. Love feasts were generally
held from Saturday afternoon through Sunday noon, so
that accomodations were needed for those coming from a
distance. Lofts of meetinghouses were also used for this
purpose. It was customary for many Brethren, lay members as well as ministers, to travel to take part in the love
feasts of other congregations, thus helping to preserve the
fellowship so emphasized by the Brethren faith. Although
the Brethren had no elaborate church *polity, such as the
Methodist system with bishops and assigned circuits for
traveling preachers, they achieved some of the same
values by the custom of periodic visits to isolated Brethren
and preaching wherever opportunity presented itself.

Brethren church government was never strictly congregational. All important church actions required the
presence and assistance of representatives of the larger
brotherhood. As previously described, congregations
were organized under the guidance of visiting elders,
ministers were called to office in their presence, and
serious matters of church discipline were decided with
their aid. When the counsel of these *"adjoining elders"
could not settle an issue, it was taken to the highest level,
the *Annual Meeting. Such questions, called *queries
after Quaker (*Society of Friends) practice, were carefully
noted and answered. These decisions were circulated in
writing to all congregations for the guidance of members.
After 1837 minutes were printed in German and English
for greater ease in distribution.

The Annual Meeting (or "big meeting") was said to
have been initiated in 1742 because of the challenge

presented by the *Moravian Church under Count *Zinzendorf. Under his leadership a series of meetings (*Pennsylvania Synods) were held in 1742-43 for members of the
German-speaking religious denominations in Pennsylvania. Brethren representatives attended the early
synods but left after they came to reject what they considered to be Zinzendorf's predominance and after some
Indian converts were baptized in a manner other than
trine immersion. The Brethren meeting of 1742 was called,
it was said, to counter the Moravian initiative. Two
Brethren joined the Moravian cause in Pennsylvania,
went with them to Europe, and returned to Pennsylvania.
One, *Andreas Frey, became an outspoken critic of the
Moravians; the other, *Joseph Müller, remained with the
Moravians and sought to enlist other Brethren. A large
meeting of Brethren elders issued a strong letter of denun-
ciation and a counter-appeal to Müller to return to the
Brethren.

Brethren, according to contemporary accounts, pros-
pered economically in their new homeland and their
numbers increased. Yet, they remained quite isolated
from American society. This became painfully apparent
during the American *Revolutionary War. Brethren
refused on many counts to support the revolution. As a
*nonresistant people they could not countenance violence
and bloodshed. They or their parents had affirmed allegiance to the British crown upon their arrival in North
America; they were thankful to the crown for the religious
freedom offered them. Moreover, those men leading the
revolutionary cause were generally unfavorable to Brethren church interests. In 1775 Brethren and Mennonite
leaders issued a *"Short and Sincere Declaration" addressed
to the Pennsylvania Assembly explaining why they could
not give assistance to the revolutionary cause. Brethren
tried to stay aloof from the conflict but were not permitted to do so. The newly constituted state governments and
the national body demanded oaths of *allegiance and

*military service. Failure to comply with these demands brought accusations of treason and various penalties. Taxes were levied manifold on objectors. Many Brethren were mistreated because of their loyalty to the British.

In 1778-79 Annual Meeting urged members not to take loyalty oaths to the new regimes. Brethren were not free to provide military *substitutes in case of conscription but were excused when they hired substitutes under duress. Although it was thought best to pay taxes, those who conscientiously objected to paying for war received support from the Annual Meeting of 1781.

The family hardest hit by the revolution was the Sauer family, printers in Germantown. Although *J. Christoph Sauer I was never a member of the Brethren, he was closely sympathetic to their concerns and his son *Christopher Sauer II was a Brethren elder. Two grandsons, *Christopher Sauer III and *Peter Sauer, were outright British supporters. Sauer III was a leading broker of military intelligence for the British general staff. When Christopher Sauer II joined his sons in Philadelphia during the city's occupation by the British army, he was declared a traitor by the Pennsylvania authorities. When he returned to his large home and printing establishment in Germantown, he was arrested, brutally mistreated, and held in military imprisonment. Upon his release, he suffered the loss of his extensive personal property and real estate, down to bottles of medicine which were seized and auctioned off, leaving him in poverty.

Christopher Sauer III was a key figure in liaison between loyalist-minded Brethren and Mennonites and the British leaders. After the war ended Sauer successfully claimed compensation in England for losses suffered. He was made king's printer and assistant postmaster at St. John in *New Brunswick, Canada. Sauer died in Baltimore in 1799 while visiting his brother Samuel.

Despite their generally withdrawn posture during the colonial period, the Brethren did engage in some publication. An early book was *Das kleine Davidische Psalter-spiel (The Small Davidic Psaltery)* of 1744, a hymnal for use by Brethren and others. In 1747 the Brethren issued *Ein geringer Schein (A Humble Gleam)*, presenting views on the Scriptures and church *ordinances. Alexander Mack, Jr., wrote an *Apologie* (1788) or defense of Brethren doctrine and practices.

WESTWARD MOVEMENT. The early national period has often been described as the "dark ages" or wilderness period of Brethren history. In fact it was a richly creative period when Brethren pushed across the continent, establishing settlements on the West Coast by mid-century, preserved substantial unity despite several *schisms, and originated forms of church government and practice which are perpetuated by Brethren bodies in the 20th century. Many details of the story are still being uncovered, but enough is known to sketch at least the broad patterns of development.

A few Brethren were sufficiently disenchanted with the results of the American Revolution to abandon the new United States in order to live under British rule. These went to what later became *Ontario in *Canada. Most Brethren remained in the USA, with many joining the wave of westward *migration and settlement. Some went through Pittsburgh following the Ohio River into *Kentucky, *Ohio, and *Indiana. Others used the Cumberland Gap to reach this region. Later, some followed the northerly route using the newly created Erie Canal (1825) into the states of the old Northwest Territory (Ohio, Indiana, *Illinois, Michigan, and *Wisconsin).

The first settlement of Brethren in Kentucky was along the Hinkston Creek in 1789. A number of Brethren linked with the *Universalist movement had settled in Cape Girardeau Co., MO, by 1810. The earliest Ohio settlement seems to have been in Stone Lick (Clermont Co.) in the late 18th century. Southwestern Ohio was an area with early Brethren concentration, especially west and north of

Dayton in Montgomery and adjoining counties; by 1850 there were fifteen congregations there. Northeastern Ohio attracted enough Brethren settlers that in 1822 the first Annual Meeting held west of the Allegheny Mountains took place near Mahoning.

The exodus of the *Wolfe family has been used to epitomize Brethren migration. From a settlement in Western Fayette Co., PA, *George Wolfe I and his family traveled by river flatboat in 1800 to Logan Co., KY. His son *George Wolfe II, with a brother Jacob and others, moved north and west into the Illinois wilderness, where George Wolfe II became a leading citizen in Union and Adams Cos. *George Wolfe III traveled to *California by way of Panama in 1856 and became a church patriarch there.

Even earlier settlements took place in the Pacific Northwest. The Weigle family reached the *Oregon Territory in 1850. A generalization holds true that the wave of western settlement first reached the west coast, then filled in the trans-Mississippi west. Lack of rainfall and the absence of forests on the Great Plains made them initially less attractive for settlers bent on agricultural opportunities. Later settlement reached into the Southwest, with a lesser degree of permanence. With the completion of the transcontinental *railroads after 1869, large-scale *colonization took place in such states as *North Dakota, *Idaho, *Montana, Washington, and California. Some Brethren elders were employed by railroad companies to encourage mass Brethren colonization.

The steadiest Brethren growth came through the process of converting children of members. The covenant and brotherhood form of church followed by Brethren stressed the teaching of religion in the home, buttressed by the local congregation. A common pattern was for a number of church houses to be built for a single large congregation, to make worship services more accessible to members during that time of difficult transportation. Ordinarily members attended church services once a month at the closest meetinghouse and visited with nearby Brethren families on other Sundays. Often these church houses became separate congregations. A typical parent church congregation spawned a large number of independent, self-supporting congregations, which, in turn, often had their own congregational offspring. The Conestoga, PA, congregation of the colonial period had grown by 1908 into twenty such "daughter" or "granddaughter" congregations with five thousand members, despite repeated migration of members elsewhere.

The story was not solely one of growth. Brethren lost substantial numbers to rival denominations or suffered schisms. Because Brethren frowned on *revivalistic techniques, some members joined the more lively *Brethren in Christ, Church of God (Winebrennerian, later known as *Churches of God, General Eldership), or *Evangelical Association. As Brethren had long held a belief in universal restoration, members were open to the call of the active Universalist movement after the Revolutionary War. In South Carolina entire congregations went over to the Universalists. A study of Universalism in the South showed that the roots of the movement lay in the Brethren Universalists of the Carolinas. Universalists were also active among Brethren settlements in Kentucky, *Missouri, and Illinois, with many Brethren converts.

In the Ohio Valley, however, the greatest losses came from the upsurge of the *Restorationist movement (*Disciples of Christ) led by *Alexander Campbell and *Barton W. Stone. Large numbers of Brethren in Kentucky and southern Indiana joined this movement; *Joseph Hostetler, *Peter Hon, and *John Wright were key agents in the shift.

The 19th century saw a number of small schisms among the Brethren. The Shoemakerites, *Brethren in Christ, *Honites, Landisites (*Christian Brethren), *Leedy Brethren, Lemonites (*Free Will Dunkers), and

*Bowman Brethren were nicknames given to the divisions, derived from the names of the leaders. A larger division took place in Indiana in 1848, when *Peter Eyman and others led followers into the *Church of God (New Dunkers). This movement continued until 1962. A small number followed *W. C. Thurman with his millennial predictions in the 1860s and 1870s. A potentially serious division was averted when the *Far Western Brethren under George Wolfe II were kept within the Brethren fold. A substantial reconciliation of the Illinois-based group took place in 1859.

POLITY AND PRACTICE. During the first half of the 19th century, Brethren developed many of the patterns of church government and practice which persisted into the 20th century. The three *degrees of ministry were elaborated: *ministers in the first and second degrees and *elders. *Deacons and *deaconesses also filled leadership roles. Annual Meeting minutes detail the steps and level of increasing responsibility. Ministerial offices were ordinarily entered into in middle age and held for life. It was understood that church leadership was entrusted to men and that women were to keep silent in church. An exception was *Sarah Righter Major of Pennsylvania and Ohio. She was never recognized as a minister but was given tacit permission to preach.

The elder's office was demanding, for it entailed considerable travel. Those elected worked to maintain unity in a brotherhood that was expanding across the continent. A beloved example of the 19th-century leader was *John Kline of Virginia. He covered more than 100,000 miles, mostly on horseback. His repeated journeys did much to plant the church in what became West Virginia. The "walking evangelist" *Jacob Leatherman tramped some 20,000 miles in Maryland to fill more than 3,000 preaching engagements during his 56 years of ministry. Sacrificial labor of wives and children, who maintained the homes and farms, made such ministry possible.

Annual Meetings became more highly organized. *Standing Committee members were delegated from districts, created after 1856. The earlier method of agreement by *consensus was changed to that of voting in 1849, with two-thirds plurality of the delegates required for passage. The Annual Meeting was held at Pentecost each spring. Beginning times varied from several days before Pentecost with inclusion of Pentecost Sunday to beginning on Pentecost and continuing for several days until business was concluded. Large numbers attended these sessions, usually held on members' farms. Railroad companies at times laid spur tracks directly to meeting sites. Hundreds of non-Brethren attended to observe the deliberations and to listen to the many sermons preached. Congregations volunteered for the honor of hosting the conferences although it was a major undertaking to care for up to ten thousand people. Lists have been preserved of the quantities of foodstuffs needed to provide meals for visitors, served without charge for many years.

INNOVATIONS AND DIVISIONS. After 1850 new developments both strengthened the work of the church and introduced tension and strain. These included Brethren periodicals (*publishing), *academies and colleges (*higher education), *Sunday schools, foreign and home *missions, revival meetings, agitation for supported ministers, and questions about the necessity of a prescribed form of *dress. The manner of dress or "garb" was carefully regulated in Annual Meeting minutes during the 19th century. Prior to this Brethren were known to dress simply but with less regimentation. Some believe that Brethren were influenced by the plain dress of the Quakers; others suggest that the Brethren simply retained an archaic form of German costume.

*Henry Kurtz, a German-born former Lutheran minister, became the pioneer Brethren publisher when he issued *The Monthly Gospel Visitor in 1851 after two comparable but short-lived attempts in the 1830s. The

Gospel Visitor was a private venture printed at his farm near Poland, OH, and met with initial reservation and disapproval. It was finally permitted by Annual Meeting action of 1853. Intended by publisher Kurtz as a medium of unity and instruction, its columns were gradually opened to those who urged the Brethren to use more modern means to inculcate Brethren understandings of the gospel.

*Educational institutions were debated in the journal. Contributors pointed out that sons and daughters of the Brethren were already attending academies and colleges sponsored by other religious bodies and were in danger of being lost to the brotherhood. Critics answered that such schools would open the church to worldliness and could supplant the family and congregation as the primary places of religious teaching. The first known Brethren-run school was Jacob Miller's *select school in Bedford Co., PA, in 1852, which ceased on Miller's death in 1853. The oldest school still active in 1980, which became known as *Juniata College, was established in 1876 as the Huntingdon Normal School. The later decades of the 19th century saw a flurry of school foundings by Brethren, most of which failed or were merged with others.

Kurtz was joined in the editorship of the *Visitor* in 1855 by *James Quinter, who became a leading churchman. After Kurtz retired as editor, Quinter assumed the responsibility and then purchased the paper. Another helper of Kurtz was *Henry R. Holsinger, who went on in 1865 to found *The Christian Family Companion*, the first weekly periodical for the Brethren. Like Kurtz and Quinter, Holsinger wanted progress for the church but was more aggressive in his policies. He allowed great freedom to contributors in his paper in an open forum or rostrum; these authors and Holsinger himself were often openly critical of current church practices. His editorial policies brought such criticism from Annual Meeting that he sold the paper to Quinter. This combined paper was merged again with a publication of two brothers, *H. B.

Brumbaugh and *J. B. Brumbaugh, which in turn was united with western papers to create *The Gospel *Messenger* in 1883. Holsinger developed another periodical, *The Progressive Christian*, as a platform for his reform views. By 1876 there were ten papers published by and for the Brethren. They served to focus points of view and also developed some spirit of factionalism. The voice for the traditional wing of the Brethren was *The Vindicator*, begun in 1870. Its first editor was *Samuel Kinsey, son-in-law of *Peter Nead, the foremost doctrinal writer of the 19th century among the Brethren.

Sunday schools began to appear in Brethren congregations by the midpoint of the 19th century, often against the wishes of the older leaders who considered them to be worldly innovations. Annual Meeting in 1857 ruled that they were permissible if "conducted in gospel order." By 1852 agitation began for more activity in home and foreign missions. Repeated efforts at establishing policy and framework for these endeavors came to the Annual Meetings with little practical result. It was by district initiative in Illinois that the first foreign missionaries were sent to *Denmark in 1876. Opponents were distrustful of the money-raising efforts and organizational changes which support for such ministries would entail and suggested that there were still great needs at home which could be met with traditional methods.

Brethren had long resisted the use of revival methods, such as the *"protracted" or extended series of meetings and were suspicious of the emotionalism inherent in revival preaching. Joining the church was a serious and sobor decision, affecting one's entire future life, and should not be made under pressure, they believed. In the late 1870s, however, this type of preaching was introduced. An outstanding exponent was *S. H. Bashor, who began preaching at age twenty-three. He was credited with the conversion of ten thousand people across the nation between 1874 and 1882.

As these currents of change and debate agitated the Brethren in the 1860s and 1870s many wished to strengthen the authority of Annual Meeting to make it a true legislative body, with power to bring dissidents into line. The method used was to pass decisions at the Annual Meeting and then send committees of elders to visit local congregations to settle problems and to enforce the counsel of the meeting. At times this worked well, and factions accepted the adjudication of the visiting brethren. In other cases it failed and even heightened tensions.

By the end of the 1870s feelings ran high in the brotherhood. There were three chief factions. The traditionalists, nicknamed the *"Old Orders," had their stronghold in the *Miami Valley of Ohio. The liberals, nicknamed the *Progressives," saw Henry Holsinger as their spokesman. Those in the middle, called "Conservatives," attempted to balance the appeals from right and left and were chiefly concerned to keep church unity. In 1881 perhaps four to five thousand of the Old Order left the church which they could no longer control, taking the name Old German Baptist Brethren. They wished to follow the old ways and were opposed to the innovations which had entered the church since 1850. In a number of congregations there was contention over use of the church buildings. When a committee of Annual Meeting refused to accept the arrangements made for their hearing at the Berlin congregation, a congregation led by Holsinger, he and his followers were disfellowshiped. The Annual Meeting of 1882 upheld the committee's action, leading to the organization in 1882-83 of the Brethren Church, with perhaps five to six thousand adherents. The larger middle group, continuing the official name *German Baptist Brethren* and numbering nearly 60,000, still contained within its ranks those leaning toward conservativism and those leaning toward progressivism.

The *Civil War, or War Between the States, had not succeeded in dividing Brethren as it had most other religious bodies. This was because the Brethren, both those living in the South and those in the North, had opposed slaveholding and favored the preservation of the union, while avoiding political activity. Brethren in the South suffered more intensely from war-related events than those in the North but were supported by the northern Brethren during and after the war, both spiritually and materially.

Thus it was the case that whereas external strains and pressures had not succeeded in causing major division among the Brethren, internal tensions resulted in sad fragmentation in the early 1880s.

Old German Baptist Brethren, the ultra-conservative branch of the Brethren heritage with historical roots in the Brethren *Old Order movement of the late 19th century. The fellowship has, since the 1880s, adapted to cultural influences with cautious consideration. Today these Brethren remain somewhat aloof from society while maintaining strong spiritual and social ties among themselves.

ORIGINS: The Old Order movement developed among *German Baptist Brethren concurrently with the *Progressive Brethren movement and the two proved mutually incompatible. The Old Order movement initially had greater influence over the Annual Meeting but during the eighth decade of the 19th century the latter gradually exerted a greater influence. The newly developing Brethren periodicals gave expression to the various influences at work within the church, *The Vindicator being the voice of the Old Order cause. As polarization developed and issues began to take shape, it was apparent that certain geographical areas were stronger centers of Old Order influence. These included *Maryland, se. *Pennsylvania, the *Miami Valley of *Ohio, and *Iowa, with scattered interest throughout the denomination.

The first actual withdrawal was that of the Beaverdam, MD, congregation in 1880, with support from Pipe Creek, MD, and Antietam and Mill Creek, PA. The group held its own *council meeting at Pentecost, 1881, corresponding to the Annual Meeting. Several *Iowa congregations also organized in 1880, and the Bear Creek congregation of sw. Ohio was out of Brethren fellowship in the same year.

The actions in southern Ohio followed several *petitions to Annual Meeting from elders' conferences in the Miami Valley in 1868, 1869, 1879, and 1880. The *Resolutions Passed at the Special Conference* (1881), drawn up at a meeting held Aug. 24, 1881, in the Ludlow-Painter Creek congregation of Darke Co., OH, also resulted in withdrawal. An organizational meeting was held in the Salem congregation, Montgomery Co., OH, in Dec., 1881; the First Annual Meeting of the Old German Baptist Brethren was held in the Wolf Creek congregation of Montgomery Co. in 1882. The Maryland-Pennsylvania fellowship soon identified with the Miami Valley Brethren as did the *Virginia Brethren, and subsequently individuals or parts of congregations elsewhere identified with the Old German Baptist Brethren by endorsing the *Resolutions* of 1881.

Congregational separations and reorganizations occurred mostly in the 1880s but also continued into the 1890s. Major strength by 1900 was concentrated in Virginia, *West Virginia, Maryland, Pennsylvania, Ohio, *Indiana, *Illinois, *Missouri, *Michigan, Iowa, and *Kansas, with lesser support in *North Carolina, *Tennessee, *Nebraska, *Washington, *Idaho, *Oregon, and *California. In the interest of the new cause *The Brethren's Reasons* (1883) was published to explain the Old Order stand; *The Vindicator* was adopted as the official Old German Baptist publication; and the *Collected Annual Meeting Minutes* (1886) were revised to harmonize with the ancient practices of the church as understood by the Old German Baptist Brethren. Elders were sent by the Annual Meeting (OGBB) throughout the brotherhood to hold explanation meetings and to strengthen the new fellowship.

The initial geographic distribution left many Brethren

isolated; their welfare became the concern of elders who traveled among the congregations to minister to their spiritual needs. Many of the smaller congregations have declined over the years as gradual migration led to greater concentrations in fewer areas. During this time, however, there was considerable interest in *colonization with varying degrees of success. Congregations now (1980) extinct existed in Michigan, *Wisconsin, *North Dakota, *Wyoming, *Colorado, and *Oklahoma. Old Order congregations in *Florida have enjoyed greater success and California has been a major area of growth. There was brief interest near Rio Verde, Goias, Brazil, in the 1970s and more recently interest in *Mississippi and Washington. Distributed in fifteen states and *Ontario, the fifty-three congregations in 1980 were most concentrated in Ohio (fifteen congregations), Indiana (nine), Kansas (five), California (five), Virginia (four), and Pennsylvania (three). Reported membership at the end of 1980 was 5,091.

BELIEFS AND PRACTICES: Theologically, the Old German Baptist Brethren recognize the depravity of fallen humanity and the redemptive work of God through his son Jesus Christ. They stress the need for *repentance, public *confession, and the obedience of the penitent in a life of righteousness. They, therefore, stress *salvation by *grace, faith, and a life of obedient works as defined by the Scriptures as they understand them. They cannot understand an effectual faith without an obedient life and the manifestation of fruitful works. This, coupled with a literal interpretation of the Scriptures by the Old German Baptist Brethren, leads to the practice of certain *ordinances, including *baptism, *feetwashing, the *love feast meal, the *communion of bread and cup, the salutation of the holy *kiss, and *anointing of the sick for healing. In addition they share the other traditional Brethren doctrines, including *nonresistance, *nonconformity to the world, the sanctity of the *marriage vow, and a refusal to swear *oaths. These they hold with a rather strict uniformity which has led some to describe them as legalistic. This impression has been fostered, perhaps, by the maintenance of strong Annual Meeting and local church council meeting *authority as a safeguard against the loss of the principles mentioned above. In actual fact, some of the Old German Baptist Brethren tend to be legalistic in their interpretation of Scriptures and church council decisions and some tend to take more liberty. The result, however, has been a rather comfortable and united fellowship within the grace-faith-obedience framework.

Divisions on doctrinal points have been few, but the doctrines of divine election and *eternal security have been felt especially on the West Coast and have had an effect on traditional Old German Baptist Brethren thought there with a resultant loss of numbers (*Ripon, CA). A schism over the *charismatic movement was experienced in the Midwest in the 1960s, although it had no lasting influence within the main body.

Baptism is held by the Brethren to be for remission of sins and the witness of a clear conscience before others. It is administered on request of the applicant and after examination and instruction by the church. The rite of immersion is practiced outdoors in flowing water.

The love feast follows a *deacons' visit and begins with the self-examination (*preparatory) service. Feetwashing follows in the *"double mode" in which members go two by two, one washing and the other wiping the feet of a third person. There follows the love feast meal consisting of meat, bread, soup, and water taken in silence and meditation. Next follows the salutation of the holy kiss and finally the communion of the *unleavened bread and the cup consisting of fermented *wine.

The most obvious manifestation of the Brethren's nonconformity is their uniformity of *dress. Men can be recognized by their black broadbrim *hats, *plain "frock" coats with "stand-up collars, and broadfall pants. Most of the men wear *beards but shave their upper lips. Women can be recognized by their dark *bonnets, white *prayer coverings (*caps), and long dresses with matching *capes over the shoulders and matching aprons. Upon meeting one another (except on the street and in public places) the salutation is always the handshake and the holy kiss exchanged brother to brother and sister to sister.

Old Order meetinghouses are *architecturally simple. There are often separate doors for the brethren and sisters. Men usually sit on one side and women on the other. The benches face the front of the meetinghouse, where a long table provides seating for the *deacons on one side and the elders and ministers on the other side, facing the congregation.

The Annual Meeting is held at Pentecost, rotating among the Eastern, Ohio, Indiana, and Western districts. The meeting lasts from Saturday through Tuesday, with a love feast on Pentecost night and a general brotherhood council meeting on Tuesday. The council and dining *tents are erected on a farm and the local congregation that hosts the meeting provides lodging and other necessities.

The general doctrines and practices of the Old German Baptist Brethren have not changed significantly since the 1880s. Brethren receive a great deal of satisfaction from the fact that a love feast in the late 20th century corresponds closely to those in the recollections of the elderly members who attended their first love feast seventy years before. These elderly persons recount hearing their fathers describe similar love feasts when they, in turn, were young.

SOCIETY AND CULTURE: The Old German Baptist Brethren church was born out of a changing denomination. Proponents of the Old Order cause saw merit in maintaining the scriptural interpretations arrived at by their forefathers. There was not always a uniformity of thought among the earlier Brethren, but limited transportation and communication made the lack of uniformity less evident. With the development of Brethren *publishing and increased travel, the dissimilarities began to manifest themselves. "Progressivism" became an influence in the church and the proponents of the Old Order movement sought increasingly for a unification of thought and practice. The Old German Baptist Brethren fellowship which resulted held as one of its basic tenets that as much as possible the body of Christ should be of one mind, serving the Lord. Changes in subsequent years have thus been minimal.

As Old German Baptist Brethren have attempted to maintain their identity in a changing world, it has been evident from time to time that society has had significant influences upon them. These cultural influences have been met by the Brethren with caution and care. There is an inclination to resist the acceptance of anything new until it has been discussed in the Annual Meeting and approved by the church as it meets in council. To be sure, there are always those who more readily utilize a specific technical advance and there are those who rather adamantly resist anything new. The larger body of Brethren, however, acts as a check and balance, weighing the utility of an innovation and accepting or refusing it at a time which seems appropriate. This sometimes has led to sharp disagreements, even division, among the Brethren. In general, though, the Brethren have accepted technological advances (e.g., *electricity, *telephones, *automobiles) according to their practical application in everyday life. Such things as *radio and *television they have refused to permit in their homes, a decision which undoubtedly has been a help to the Brethren in maintaining separation from the world, a principle they hold to be precious. It also permits time for visiting and fellowshiping with other families and for reading and meditation.

Annual Meeting remains an important factor in the continued strength of the Old German Baptist Brethren.

It provides a forum for the general discussion of issues of interest to the church and lends authority to decisions which are made there. In addition it provides annually an opportunity for brotherhood fellowship and social exchange.

While *agriculture is still an important way of life, in many areas of the church, along with society in general, there has been a trend among the Brethren toward skills and crafts and occasionally to professions not traditional among the Old German Baptist Brethren. The mobility of the nonagricultural society (forty-hour week and leisure time on weekends) has permitted Brethren to enjoy fellowship across the nation, and it is common for Brethren to travel from state to state on weekends to attend worship services. This has led to a greater social and spiritual interchange which strengthens and unifies the Brethren even more as cultural change exerts its pressures upon them. Increasing financial security (which is rather general among the Old German Baptist Brethren) has had an expected effect upon the *simple life-style which had characterized the Brethren in the past.

*Educational institutions operated by the Brethren were specifically forbidden among the Old Orders as a primary tenet of the *Resolutions* of 1881. In addition the Brethren have more or less resisted high school and college education. Since the 1940s, however, and perhaps largely as a result of the move away from the farm, high school and selected professional institutions have been cautiously recognized in most areas as not inconsistent with the Old German Baptist life-style. In addition, recognizing the unfavorable influences in the public schools, in 1979 Annual Meeting permitted the Brethren to operate private schools for the education of their own children. Several of these schools have been established (*Christian day school movement). In 1980 it would seem premature to attempt to evaluate the influences of these various educational endeavors upon the church.

Significant geographic and individual variation in thought and practice is minimized among the Brethren by their tendency to make comparisons among themselves both as to the externals (e.g., uniformity of dress, model and color of automobile, interior decorations in their homes — or the absence of such) and the intangibles (e.g., interpretation of the Scriptures, conservatism or liberality of thought). In certain cases there has been a tendency for the more conservative Brethren to move to a congregation where they feel comfortable among those of similar thought and for the more progressive to do likewise. While this has at times led to greater polarity, in general it seems to have contributed to a course of moderation throughout the church.

The influence of personalities within the fellowship is recognized, taking into account a variety of abilities. In the selection of a minister or a deacon, for instance, each member must make a choice from among those who seem to show ability, genuineness, and spiritual maturity. When selecting one to the Standing Committee, preference is given to one who has shown evidence of leadership ability and a leaning toward moderation, one who holds the general respect of his peers and the church. When one is called to serve the church in special ways, tears and hesitation are often manifest, but submission to the responsibility of the calling follows. Whether there is hesitancy or not, the will of the individual is subject to the larger brotherhood.

DIVISION AND GROWTH: Several divisions have occurred among the Old German Baptist Brethren. The first division occurred in 1913, primarily in the area of Camden, IN. In 1980 this fellowship, called the *Old Brethren, is strongest at Wakarusa, IN, Salida and Twaine Harte, CA, and Gettysburg, OH. The Old Brethren also have a small congregation at Maple, Ontario, and have made ventures into Mississippi and Brazil. The primary causes for division in 1913 were the adoption of the telephone and automobile which the Old Brethren originally had rejected. The Old Brethren publish a monthly paper called *The Pilgrim. The casual observer in 1980 would notice little difference between the Old German Baptist Brethren and the Old Brethren originating in 1913. However, the latter encourage a more congregational method of applying *discipline and do not favor a strong central authority through their Annual Meeting.

A subdivision of the Old Brethren developed about 1930, once more over the question of the automobile, which the main body of Old Brethren by this time had accepted. The dissenting group, which became known as the *Old Brethren German Baptists, is concentrated in the Camden, IN, area. Members still refuse to use automobiles, telephones, and electricity. They are one of the two Brethren fellowships to use horse-drawn *buggies.

The second division of the Old German Baptist Brethren occurred in 1921 in Miami Co., OH, with followers from surrounding counties and from Indiana, Maryland, and Kansas. Known as the *Old Order German Baptist Brethren, this group has two meetinghouses in Miami and Darke Cos., OH. The division occurred over the use of the automobile, members continue to use horses and buggies for transportation and use neither electricity nor telephones in their homes. Their doctrine and ordinances are essentially the same as the Old German Baptist Brethren and they favor a strong Annual Meeting authority.

A local division of the Old German Baptist Brethren occurred in Greene and Montgomery Cos., OH, in 1946 over the authority of the Annual Meeting, a controversy precipitated by the use of the radio. This group, called the Old German Baptist Brethren of Greene County, OH, became extinct in the 1960s.

Finally, in the 1960s a movement of a different nature developed in the lower Miami Valley which resulted in the inspirationist or charismatic group called *Christ's

Assembly. Organized in 1967 by *Johannes Thalitzer (Hansen) of the Christ's Assembly in Denmark (Christi Meneghed), it was also influenced by the 18th-century teachings of *J. Conrad Beissel of the *Ephrata Community and the *Community of True Inspiration. Members practice the Pentecostal spirit, Brethren ordinances, Inspirationist "revelations," and celibacy. Glossolalia and divine physical healing are also a part of their teachings. In 1980 the group was declining in numbers.

Fairly accurate growth records have been kept among the Old German Baptist Brethren in the later part of the 20th century. Membership in 1980 was 5,091 in 53 congregations, representing a 21 percent growth since 1965. The rate of growth for these 15 years increases from the West to the East Coast with the state growth rates as follows: California 11 percent, Kansas 19 percent, Indiana 18 percent, Ohio 22 percent, Pennsylvania 28 percent, Virginia 37 percent. The smaller and more geographically isolated congregations had a collective growth rate of 21 percent (including Oregon, Missouri, Illinois, Michigan, West Virginia, North Carolina, Florida, and Ontario). Suburban areas showed slower growth rate or, in a few cases, decline. Only five congregations of significant size showed losses, including three congregations which were discontinued (two urban and one rural). Two new congregations were formed during these fifteen years, one suburban and one rural. In 1980, a third new congregation was formed in rural Mississippi. The average annual growth rate from 1965 to 1980 was 1.4 percent compared to the national population growth of 1.2 percent per annum. The Old Brethren and the Old Order German Baptist Brethren also were growing.

SUMMARY: The Old German Baptist Brethren church and related Old Order groups represent an adaptation of mid-19th century Brethren thought and practice to the late 20th century. Continual effort has been made to preserve the old ways as handed down from one generation to the next. Adaptations to cultural change and technical developments have not been made without serious thought, although sometimes leading to unfortunate division. Old Order Brethren make material contributions to society in agriculture, especially in the areas of produce, orchards, corn, grain, and livestock. Brethren also work in construction, manufacturing, and the medical profession. While Old Order Brethren support no evangelistic missionary movement, there is continued growth through the enlargement of existing congregations. New congregations continue to be formed and migration to new areas is occurring.

Brethren Church, The, with headquarters in Ashland, OH, one wing of the *Progressive Brethren movement of the 1870s and 1880s. With a membership of 15,485 in the USA (1980), the 123 Brethren Church congregations are most heavily concentrated in Indiana, Ohio, and Pennsylvania. Most congregations conduct *Sunday (church) school on Sunday morning, worship services Sunday morning and evening, a midweek prayer service or Bible study, and have one or more auxiliary organizations (most frequently the *Woman's Missionary Society). Congregational business (*council) meetings are presided over by a moderator, who is usually not a minister or elder, and the work of the congregation is administered by an official board. The latter usually includes congregational officers, church school leaders, representatives of auxiliaries, trustees and deacons or their representatives, committee chairmen or chairwomen, and the pastor. Local church membership in 1980 averaged 126, average Sunday morning worship attendance was 87.

Congregations are clustered geographically into nine districts, each of which holds an annual conference. District conferences effect their own organization somewhat along the lines of the General Conference (see below), providing at their level for such concerns as they are able (e.g., district missionary boards).

The General Conference of the Brethren Church meets each year in Ashland, OH, for fellowship, inspiration, and denominational business. The delegate body is composed of all ordained ministers present and representatives from local congregations, district conferences, and the cooperating boards and auxiliary organizations of the General Conference. The General Conference controls only its own sessions and the organs created by it (i.e., boards, committees, and the establishment of auxiliaries). These are:

(1) Auxiliary organizations: Brethren Youth Crusaders (BYC), *National Laymen's Organization (NLO), and Woman's Missionary Society (WMS), each auxiliary with its own organization at local, district, and national levels as well as its own publication. The NLO sponsors the *Young Men and Boys' Brotherhood and the WMS, the *Sisterhood of Mary and Martha.

(2) Standing committees: Committee on Committees, Conference Membership, Executive Committee, Goals, Ministerial Recruitment, Nominations, Polity, Rules and Organization, Social Concerns, Spiritual State of the Churches, Stewardship, and Worship.

(3) Special committees as needed.

(4) Cooperating boards: (*a*) the *Benevolent Board, which operates *retirement homes in Ashland, OH; Flora, IN; and South Bend, IN; (*b*) the *Board of Christian Education, which concerns itself with all aspects of Christian nurture and discipleship, including the program of Brethren Youth Crusaders; (*c*) the Board of Trustees of the Retirement Fund, which administers a program of hospitalization and retirement insurance for pastors and employees of General Conference boards; (*d*) the *Brethren Publishing Company, which produces *The Brethren Bible Class Quarterly* (adult studies following the *International Lesson Series curriculum), *The Brethren Evangelist* (the monthly denominational magazine), and other literature; (*e*) the *Missionary Board, which oversees church planting and development in *Argentina, *Colombia, *India, *Malaysia, *Mexico, and the USA; (*f*) the *World Relief Board, which

cooperates with the Church of the Brethren in domestic
*disaster relief and with the World Relief Corporation, an
agency of the *National Association of Evanglicals, to
which the General Conference belongs.

The Brethren Church sponsors but does not operate
*Ashland College and *Ashland Theological Seminary.
These are one legal entity on two campuses in Ashland,
OH. The majority of the trustees for the schools are
nominated by the district conferences of the Brethren
Church or represent the denomination at large.

BASIC PRINCIPLES. In its history the Brethren Church
has retained the vision of being true to the Scriptures as
understood by the founders of the Brethren movement.
*Henry R. Holsinger and other leaders of the Progressive
Brethren movement thought of themselves as the conser-
vators of the original Brethren ideals and interpretations,
being progressive only in the application of these ideals to
present-day life. For that purpose they were in favor of
organized *Christian education at congregational and college levels (*higher education), an educated and *salaried
ministry, open denominational *publications, and a
deliberate policy of *evangelism and *mission outreach.
They were opposed to what they believed was an un-
necessary amount of *authority given to *Annual Meeting
decisions, desiring, rather, a more congregational and
consentient mode of church government.

In the General Conferences of the first fifteen years
(1882-97) leaders adopted a series of basic principles
which continue to guide the Brethren Church. During
those years Brethren Church fortunes were tied particularly to Ashland College, which, after considerable
financial struggle, managed to remain open under the
leadership of *J. Allen Miller, president, 1898-1906.
Lingering uncertainties in *polity were resolved when *A
Manual of Procedure for the Brethren Church* was
adopted in 1915.

A *Foreign Missionary Society, which began in 1900,

sent *Charles F. and Pearl Lutz Yoder to Argentina as the first permanent placements in 1908. While the Argentine work grew slowly, a second field was opened in *Oubangui-Chari in west-central Africa by *James and *Florence Newberry Gribble, *Estella Myers, and others, 1918-21. A program of home missions also was launched during this period when *George and Ada Drushal began the *Riverside Institute at Lost Creek, KY, a school and church program that soon received support from the Missionary Board.

CONTROVERSY AND DIVISION. In the Brethren Church, as in many denominations, the first third of the 20th century was marked by controversy over *Fundamentalism, *Liberalism, Modernism, and the *Social Gospel. In this context the *National Ministerial Association (BC) accepted in 1921 a document outlining for Brethren elders the central areas of doctrine. This *"Message of the Brethren Ministry" was not adopted by the General Conference lest such action give the impression of establishing a *creed other than the New Testament for the church.

The above-mentioned controversies continued to trouble the Brethren Church, however, with the result that some ministers left the denomination during the 1920s because it seemed too conservative while others pressed for greater defenses against the threat perceived in Liberalism and Modernism. The latter group came to be led by *Louis S. Bauman and *Alva J. McClain, dean of Ashland Theological Seminary, 1933-37, who espoused a more protective stance in educational philosophy and life-style at Ashland College and a modified dispensational Fundamentalism in theology. They accused the "Ashland Brethren" of legalism, making obedience to all Christ's commands (*discipleship) appear necessary for salvation, and of Modernism, tolerating non-Brethren ideas and conduct at Ashland College. The Ashland group charged the "Grace Brethren" with ignoring the centrality of *Sermon on the Mount ethics and teaching *antinomianism in their emphasis on salvation solely by grace with its corollary of *eternal (i.e., unconditional) security.

The issues were not resolved. A power struggle involving strong personalities resulted in the division of the 1939 General Conference. The Ashland Brethren retained control of the college and seminary; the Grace Brethren (later reorganized as the National Fellowship of Grace Brethren Churches) retained the foreign missionary program and established a new seminary and college at Winona Lake, IN (*Grace Schools). Because most of the young pastors educated at Ashland under Dean McClain followed him into the Fellowship of Grace Brethren Churches, the Brethren Church lost much of its leadership for the next generation.

C. F. Yoder left his retirement to return to Argentina to begin a fresh Brethren Church mission field, and Veda Liskey went to northeastern Nigeria in cooperation with the Church of the Brethren (1948). Until ca. 1970 Ashland College experienced growth under *Glenn L. Clayton (president, 1948-77). Especially noteworthy was the work of the denomination's WMS, led by *Nora Early Shively, in raising funds for the construction of the Memorial Chapel (1952). In the mid-1950s the General Conference established a Central Planning and Coordinating Committee (*Central Council) which integrated denominational work until it was dissolved in a 1979 General Conference reorganization.

During the 1960s *Albert T. Ronk, who as a youth knew and assisted H. R. Holsinger, produced several publications for the denomination, the major one being his *History of the Brethren Church* (1968). The question of *rebaptizing transfer members previously immersed was studied and discussed at length. The General Conference of 1978 voted to allow congregations to receive as members believers previously immersed by some form other than trine immersion, if they pledged anew their faith in Jesus Christ and evidenced it in their lives. The

Conference of 1980 reaffirmed the threefold communion service (*love feast) as constitutive of the Brethren Church. Under the leadership of Joseph R. Shultz (b. 1927), Ashland Theological Seminary enjoyed growth and accreditation beginning in the mid-1960s. In 1980 Shultz was named president of Ashland College and Seminary.

BRETHREN CHURCH DOCTRINES. The doctrinal position of the Brethren Church conforms in general to a conservative Protestant or evangelical stance. The Brethren heritage is maintained in thinking of theology as not so much a system of ideas produced from a textbook as a style of life absorbed from the obedient community of faith. It is not merely to be thought about with the mind but actualized with the whole life. Brethren Church doctrine intends to center on Jesus Christ as the living Word of God and on Christianity as a way of life derived from and dependent upon him as Son of God, Savior, and Lord. He is confessed, as in classical orthodoxy, as true God and true Man, one person with two natures.

The *Bible as Holy Scripture is the written Word of God and may be understood in analogy with the living Word, Jesus Christ. That is, Scripture has both a truly divine aspect and a truly human aspect, the two to be held together. As the living Word was human, yet without sin, so the written Word is confessed to be human, yet without error. As Christ was divine, yet limited in the days of his flesh, so Scripture is confessed to be divine, yet limited in not affording all the information or certitude that sometimes might be desired.

The New Testament is considered to be the fulfullment of the Old Testament without destroying the validity of the earlier covenant. There is, as the *Anabaptists held, both continuity and discontinuity between the testaments, with the New Testament being on a higher plane in the progress of revelation because it is the fulfillment of what was promised and begun in the Old Testament. When the provision for redemption was accomplished (Jn. 19:30;

Heb. 9:26b), then the way was provided for the closing of the canon in a theological sense, for the apostles and their associates played a role of priority that no other generations can play in the witness to the Jesus of history as the Christ of faith. The statement on "The Message of the Brethren Ministry" bears testimony to the belief that "God's supreme revelation has been made through Jesus Christ, a complete and authentic record of which revelation is the New Testament; and, to the belief that the Holy Scriptures of the Old and New Testaments, as originally given, are the infallible record of the perfect, final and authoritative revelation of God's will, altogether sufficient in themselves as a rule of faith and practice."

The God revealed in these Scriptures is eternally triune, possessing many attributes, but the disclosure of them may be summarized in the phrase *holy *love*. Holiness is the background of all the divine qualities, defined as that in God's nature which distances him from his creation, especially from the rebellious creation in sin. Holiness expresses first separateness, then purity, then perfection. Love is the foreground of the divine qualities as that in God's nature which moves him toward his creation, even the sinful creation. While both summary attributes are found in both the Old and the New Testaments, holiness is the pedagogical emphasis in the Old Testament and love is the pedagogical emphasis in the New Testament. Neither is at base an emotion; both, rather, are qualities of character and hence of will. Neither cancels the other or overpowers it; together they demand satisfaction for sin and together they offer the same from within the divine nature. Thus, the New Testament exalts the grace of God which, in holy love contrary to what might be expected, provides atonement and bestows pardon (2 Cor. 8:9; Eph. 2:4-9).

The Brethren Church confesses Christ along the lines of classical western orthodoxy as set out, for example, in the Apostles' Creed, the Nicene Creed, the Athanasian

Creed, and the Chalcedonian definition (*Christology).
His deity, pre-existence, and incarnation by virgin birth
are asserted together with his humanity, exaltation, and
glorification by *resurrection and ascension. His life upon
earth is a principial model for believers, and his death
upon the cross is a full, complete atonement for sin. In the
language of the Epistle to the Hebrews, Christ both officiated as priest and offered himself as sacrifice, all done
voluntarily from within the depths of the divine mercy.

Having been raised from death and exalted to heaven,
he has sent in his place the Holy Spirit so that his disciples
will not be left orphans (Jn. 14:18). The Spirit, who is
another Paraclete (Jn. 14:16), continues to be advocate
and counselor for believers, as Christ was in the days of
his flesh. In addition, the Spirit applies the work of accomplished redemption to sinful human beings in their
present experience. He is the seal and guardian of its genuineness (Eph. 1:13-14). He gives spiritual gifts (in Greek,
charismata, or "grace-gifts") to believers: gifts of service
for meeting human needs inside and outside the church;
gifts of equipping to enable the ministries just mentioned
(Eph. 4:11-12); and sign-gifts for confirming the truth of
the gospel in its pioneering breakthroughs into new territories (Heb. 2:3-4). The Holy Spirit always acts in such a
way as to exalt Christ and never in contradiction to the
Scriptures he inspired. Thus, Holy Spirit and Holy Scripture operate together as what *Alexander Mack, Sr., called
the *inner and outer words testifying of Christ.

DOCTRINE OF SALVATION. In soteriology the Brethren
Church reflects the origins of the Brethren movement out
of several theological traditions. *Salvation is viewed as
both gift and demand (Lk. 4:14-21; Mt. 4:23-5:12; cf.
5:13-20; Lk. 14:25-33). The objective-external aspects in
justification and adoption are taught together with the
subjective-internal aspects of regeneration and union with
Christ. All of these are biblical metaphors describing and
reflecting upon entry into the Christian life. The prere-

quisite is *conversion (i.e., turning from sin in *repentance and turning to Christ in faith), which is graciously
made possible in the hearing of the gospel (Rom. 10:17).
Salvation, therefore, is open to all and is divinely intended
for all (Rom. 10:12-13; 11:32; 1 Tim. 2:4-6; 2 Pet. 3:9).

As faith obtains this salvation, so faithfulness main-
tains it. *Justification is "by personal faith in the Lord
Jesus Christ, of which obedience to the will of God and
works of righteousness are the evidence and result"
("Message of the Brethren Ministry"). Belief and obedience are convertible terms in biblical thought (Mt.
7:21-23; Jn. 3:36; Heb. 3:18-19; 2 Thess. 1:8), and *sanctification describes the entirety of "the obedience of faith"
(Rom. 1:5; 16:26). There is a positional sanctification at
conversion, a progressive sanctification throughout the
present earthly life, and a final, perfect sanctification at
death or at the return of Christ. The first of these is the
divine answer to the penalty of sin; the second, to the continuing power of sin; and the third, to the very possibility
of sin. The last does not occur during this life, lived as it is
in a fallen, rebellious world which continues to affect
believers in all aspects of their existence (Phil. 3:12-14).

This also means that the believer's security is conditional. God is faithful, and he demands faithfulness on
the part of those who are his (1 Cor. 10:1-13; Col.
1:22-23; Heb. 3:12-4:13; 6:1-15; 10:19-36). They are kept
by the power of God, which operates through their faith
(1 Pet. 1:5). Similarly, election and calling are God's
gracious work in Christ responded to by those who believe
(Lk. 7:29-30; Acts 13:46-48), who are elect (chosen) according to the purpose of God (Rom. 8:28). And, as the
elect in Christ, they are predestined to be conformed to
the image of Christ (Rom. 8:29). Scripture presents such
matters as divine sovereignty and human responsibility
side by side (Rom. 9:14-18; 10:9-17), unresolved, and
often in a context of worship rather than explanation
(Rom. 11:25-36).

DOCTRINE OF THE CHURCH. In ecclesiology the Brethren Church does not view the *church in total continuity with Old Testament Israel (as in Puritanism) or in total discontinuity with Israel (as in *dispensationalism). Instead, following Anabaptism, the church is believed to be a visible community both continuous and discontinuous with Israel. The church is the fulfillment of God's plan for humanity to which Israel was called as his elect (chosen) means. Christ is the one supremely chosen by God (Isa. 42:1; 49:7; 1 Pet. 1:20; 2:4), and his church is therefore at once the people of God (a title repeatedly employed in the Old Testament), the body of Christ (a characteristically Pauline expression), and the *fellowship (communion, in Greek, *koinonia*; in German, *Gemeinschaft*) of the Holy Spirit.

Advocates of all basic forms of church polity—episcopal, presbyterian, and congregational—claim to find the roots of these polities in the New Testament. Brethren Church polity has been described as a limited or federated congregationalism; that is, local affairs may be administered in a variety of ways, but a spiritual consensus in doctrinal matters is to be sought and expected. The ordained *ministry is conducted by *elders, whose ordination is for life. Licensed ministers are on probation looking toward ordination. They may perform most pastoral tasks under supervision for a period of up to five years, except that they may not ordain elders or deacons. The latter, both *women and men, are chosen for local service, the length of which is set by the individual congregation.

ORDINANCES OF THE BRETHREN CHURCH. The major Brethren Church publication in doctrine was C. F. Yoder's study of the *ordinances, *God's Means of Grace* (1908). *Baptism is administered by trine immersion only, signifying the role of each member of the triune godhead in Christian salvation and the believer's relationship to each. Congregations, as noted above, have the privilege of receiving into membership believers previously immersed in a baptism other than trine immersion, but all Brethren Church baptisms are performed by this mode. The communion service also is a threefold rite consisting of *feetwashing, the act of cleansing and service; a common meal (in Greek, *agape*), the act of fellowship; and *eucharist, the act of thanksgiving. Normally it is held in the evening, the covered supper being on the table at the beginning of the service, the feetwashing proceeding according to the *"single mode" followed at once by the *kiss of peace, and the eucharist employing *unleavened bread and unfermented *grape juice. The menu of the meal varies from congregation to congregation.

The *laying on of hands is practiced on three occasions: at *confirmation following baptism (whether in the water, or immediately following reclothing, or at a designated later service), at *anointing with oil for the *healing of the sick, and at the *ordination of elders or deacons. The "negatives" (*nonconformity to the world, *nonresistance to evil and violence, and nonswearing of *oaths) are not emphasized so strongly as in earlier days. Their observance varies with the part of the country, the congregation involved, and the pastoral teaching received. All are acknowledged as the historic tradition of the Brethren movement, but not all Brethren Church members and leaders are agreed on the interpretation of the biblical teachings or on how to apply those teachings to present situations.

DOCTRINE OF ULTIMATE DESTINIES. Such variation carries over into *eschatology. It is universally held in the Brethren Church that Jesus Christ will return to earth in time and space and that the dead in Christ are now at rest in the Lord. The purpose of Christ's return will be to claim his bride the church, to render judgment upon the world and all its inhabitants (believers and unbelievers), and to defeat finally and forever the powers of evil. Members of the Brethren Church generally accept a premillennial interpretation of eschatology (*millen-nialism), that is, that Christ will return in order to establish perfect justice in a perfect earthly environment so that the world of people and nature may know for once in human experience what the divine purpose intended from the beginning.

As to how this might be related to "the great tribula-tion," most members of the Brethren Church (following popular Fundamentalism) hold to a pretribulation rapture of the church; there are those, however, who understand Scripture to teach a midtribulation or posttribulation coming of the Lord for his church. The "Message of the Brethren Ministry" affirms only belief in the return of Christ, making no further specifications.

As to the final state of all humanity, *heaven and *hell are affirmed to be eternal (i.e., everlasting). *Univer-salism, restorationism, and annihilationism are rejected together with belief in either conditional or temporary final states. The emphasis in eschatology is upon "the per-sonal and visible return of our Lord Jesus Christ from heaven as King of Kings and Lord of Lords, the glorious goal for which we are taught to watch, wait, and pray" ("Message of the Brethren Ministry").

Such an understanding should not lead, however, to quietism, for the biblical witness implies that eschatology leads properly to *ethics. The promise and hope of the second advent call not for speculation but for obedience in the form of Christian service (1 Cor. 15:58) and holy living (2 Pet. 3:11; 1 Jn. 3:2-3). Preparation of a new statement of doctrine was begun in conjunction with the centennial of the formation of the Brethren Church (1982-83).

Right: Alexander Mack School in Schwarzenau/ Eder, Federal Republic of Germany; it was built with gifts from members of the Church of the Brethren (BHLA). *Below:* Participants and onlookers at the 250th anniversary celebration of the founding of the Brethren movement, held at Schwarzenau/Eder on August 6, 1958 (BHLA).

Above: Two of the main buildings of the Ephrata Cloister, Ephrata, PA, ca. 1918 (Sara B. Musselman Collection). *Below:* Germantown Church of the Brethren, Philadelphia, PA (D. F. Durnbaugh Collection).

Above: Barnraising near Berlin, PA, ca. 1900 (Doris Lambert Collection).
Below: The family and farm of Daniel and Mary Jane Nock Rothenberger, near North Webster, IN, in 1897 (Dale E. Rusher Collection).

Left: Elizabeth McClanahan Royer (1836-1918) reading the Bible near Mercersburg, PA, 1917 (Kermon Thomasson Collection). *Below:* Reuel B. Pritchett at the log Meadow Branch meetinghouse, Granges Co., TN (Elgin P. Kintner Collection).

Members of the Old German Baptist Brethren at the Annual Meeting held near North Manchester, IN, in May, 1977 (Peter Michael photo).

Members of the Old German Baptist Brethren at the Annual Meeting held near North Manchester, IN, in May, 1977 (Peter Michael photo).

Above: Session of the Annual Meeting of the Old German Baptist Brethren, held near North Manchester, IN, in May, 1977 (Peter Michael photo). *Below:* View of the Annual Meeting of the Old German Baptist Brethren, in Montgomery Co., OH, at Pentecost, 1972 (Keith Sides photo; Fred W. Benedict Collection).

Left: H. R. Holsinger and Susanna Shoup Holsinger (Ashland Theological Seminary Library). *Below:* Leaders of the early Brethren Church: l-r, top row — Jonathan Swihart, Henry R. Holsinger, Edward G. Mason, Eli L. Yoder; bottom row — P. J. Brown, Stephen H. Bashor (Ashland Theological Seminary Library).

Home missionaries of the Church of the Brethren, with B. E. Kesler at left (BHLA).

Above: Conference of the Dunkard Brethren, Plevna, IN, held on June 23, 1926 (Howard J. Surbey Collection). *Below:* Spring Creek meetinghouse of the German Baptist Brethren, at Hershey, PA, in 1910 (Library, Palmyra, PA, Church of the Brethren).

Above: Gathering of the Linville Creek, VA, German Baptist Brethren, ca. 1907; M. R. Zigler is in the middle, wearing a light-colored hat (M. R. Zigler Collection). *Below:* Planting potatoes at Elizabethtown College, Elizabethtown, PA, early 20th century; H. K. Ober is in the center, wearing a hat (Elizabethtown College Library).

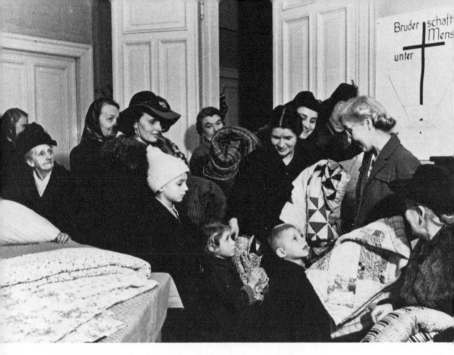

Above: Distribution of relief materials, Bremen, Germany, ca. 1947; Cecile Burke, Brethren Service Commission worker, stands at right (BHLA).
Below: Congregation and pastor of the Zion Hill Church of the Brethren, Columbiana, OH, 1971 (*Youngstown Vindicator* photo).

Above: Three leaders of the Church of the Brethren in India: l-r, Naranji V. Solanki, Premchand G. Bhagat, Govindji H. Satvedi (BHLA). *Below:* Officers of the United Nations presiding at the General Assembly, 1959; l-r, Dag Hammarskjold, U Thant, and Andrew W. Cordier, a member of the Church of the Brethren (United Nations photo).

Louis S. Bauman, leader of the Fellowship of Grace Brethren Churches (Brethren Missionary Herald Collection).

Church of the Brethren, 1883-1980. Following the *Progressive Brethren and *Old Order divisions of 1881-83, the majority "Conservative" *Brethren (German Baptist Brethren) sought to heal the wounds of separation. Approximately 4,000 Old Orders and 5,000 Progressives (Brethren Church) left the main body in the early 1880s, leaving a membership of ca. 50,000. The issues surrounding the divisions—*higher education, *Sunday schools, *missions, and *evangelism—were still present, although in a more subdued way. Because the loudest voices calling for either immediate change or strict adherence to the old *order had been silenced, the church continued the process of accommodation to the world (*acculturation), although at a pace that would not have been possible before the *Civil War. This transformation was so thoroughly "progressive" that, ironically, by 1900 many of the innovations which *H. R. Holsinger and others had so vigorously championed were more characteristic of the main body of German Baptist Brethren than the Brethren Church.

There was, for example, the matter of a more suitable name. By the late 19th century much of the leadership was convinced that the title German Baptist Brethren reflected too much of a narrow, closed, "country Dutch" background. By 1900 most Brethren could probably not read or speak German, although the last German edition hymnbook was published in 1903. Popularly the Brethren were still known as *Dunkers* or *Dunkards* (from their

70 MEET THE BRETHREN

manner of immersion *baptism), and in 1905 the *Annual Meeting nearly adopted the name "Dunker Brethren Church." Finally, in 1908—the *bicentennial of the first *Schwarzenau baptisms—Annual Meeting adopted *Church of the Brethren* as the official name, by which the denomination has been known ever since.

EVANGELISM AND MISSIONS, PUBLISHING, EDUCATION. The accommodation of the church to mainstream Protestantism is also clearly seen in activity related to evangelism, education, and publishing. Membership, after the initial loss caused by the divisions, had more than recovered by 1900 and stood at ca. 75,000. Much of this increase resulted from the widespread practice of holding *revival meetings. Such popular evangelists as *I. N. H. Beahm, *I. J. Rosenberger, and *H. C. Early traveled widely holding *protracted meetings and baptizing hundreds of people. In the late 20th century many congregations continue to hold annual or semiannual revival services.

Another method of encouraging church growth was through *colonization efforts. Working with *railroads and *land companies, numerous Brethren, including *A. B. Peters and *M. M. Eshelman, became involved in plans to develop agricultural colonies in several western states. Such efforts had the greatest impact in *North Dakota, *California, *Idaho, and *Washington, where scores of new congregations were started between 1890 and 1910. Controversy developed, however, because the programs frequently left the older mid-Atlantic and mid-western congregations much reduced in numbers. Also, Brethren in the West frequently moved from location to location, leaving newly organized churches in unstable condition. Still others questioned the ethics of church leaders who stood to gain financially by colonization efforts.

The late 19th century also witnessed several attempts by *districts and individuals to initiate mission activity in industrial centers (*urban ministry). Most notable were city missions in Baltimore, Brooklyn, Pittsburgh, Chicago, St. Louis, Kansas City, and Los Angeles. Although a few developed into permanent congregations, in the mid-20th century most Brethren families lived on farms or in small towns.

It was in the area of foreign missions, however, that late 19th- and early 20th-century Brethren showed their greatest zeal for evangelism. Indeed, many insisted that this missionary activity was the single most important ministry of the church. The first efforts, however, in *Denmark (1876) and *India (1894) began modestly enough. When the first missionary board, the *Foreign and Domestic Missionary Board, was created in 1884 it had fewer than ten dollars in its treasury. Receipts at the end of that year were slightly more than $3,500. By 1913 the General Mission Board had assets of nearly one million dollars. Much of the credit for organizing and popularizing the work of foreign missions was the result of efforts by *D. Vaniman, *D. L. Miller, and *W. B. Stover. Vaniman was the major architect of the mission boards of the church. Miller, a wealthy businessman, educator, editor, and minister, greatly stimulated Brethren interest in foreign lands through published accounts of his world travels. Stover, pioneer Brethren missionary to India, through his writing and speaking tours, helped make the goal of supporting foreign mission work a high priority of many local congregations. The *Student Volunteer Movement also played an important part in *missions education.

The mission effort in India proved so successful that new fields were opened up in northern *China (1908), *Nigeria (1922), and *Ecuador (1946). Foreign mission service became the goal of many young people; the commissioning of missionaries at *missionary convocation was a high point of each Annual Conference for many years.

This enthusiasm waned in the 1950s as the mission philosophy of the denomination went through considerable change. The first major shock came in China, 1949-50, with the success of the Communist revolution. All missionaries were expelled and foreign work there terminated. In 1955 Annual Conference approved the mission strategy of creating indigenous, independent, and self-supporting churches (*Mission Guidelines). This idea was later coupled with mutuality and partnership in working with national Christian groups. Although there was criticism of these changes, they proceeded apace. In Ecuador, the Brethren congregations were founding partners of the *United Evangelical Church of Ecuador, 1965. The India mission joined the *Church of North India in 1970. In Nigeria, the largest mission field, indigenization took place in two stages. The first came with its congregations joining the *Fellowship of Churches of Christ in Nigeria (the Brethren portion of which was later called Lardin Gabas). Then in 1973 a fully independent and autonomous *Church of the Brethren in Nigeria (Ekklesiyar 'Yan'uwa a Nigeria) was created with over 30,000 members. The mutuality concept had its clearest expression in *Misión Mutua en las Américas (1975) which has sought to establish a cooperative mission effort with Latin American denominations.

Publishing, likewise, had an ever increasing impact on the life of the church. Various periodicals had helped to fuel the flames of division during the early 1880s. Yet undeniably it was *The Gospel Messenger* (published since 1965 as *Messenger*), itself a merger in 1883 of *The Primitive Christian* and *Brethren At Work*, which helped the denomination find a sense of unity. Although it had been privately owned, the periodical was transferred to the General Mission Board in 1897, following an earlier Annual Conference decision that the church should control all publishing interests. Between 1885 and 1915 the editorial team of D. L. Miller and *J. H. Moore made the paper a household word in Brethren homes. Other periodicals such as *The Missionary Visitor* and *The Inglenook* served special interests within the life of the church.

The Brethren Publishing House, begun as a private venture in 1896, moved to *Elgin, IL in 1899, but did not become independent of the mission board until 1916. Hundreds of *tracts and pamphlets describing Brethren beliefs and practices were published and distributed. Doctrinal and *devotional books by Brethren writers for Brethren readers began to appear regularly. Two of the most important books published during this period were *History of the German Baptist Brethren* (1899) by *M. G. Brumbaugh and *Literary Activity of the German Baptist Brethren* (1908) by *John S. Flory. Both Brumbaugh and Flory were among the first Brethren to earn PhD degrees and their works were intended to give the church pride in its colonial heritage.

The career of Brumbaugh also serves to illustrate additional signs of acculturation. He wore many labels—historian, governor of Pennsylvania, prohibitionist, minister, and church leader—but he was foremost an educator. Among his many offices Brumbaugh was superintendent of schools in Huntingdon Co. and Philadelphia, president of *Juniata College, 1893-1911, 1924-1930, and US Commissioner of Education in Puerto Rico, 1900-1902.

The faltering Brethren educational activity during the 1860s and 1870s burgeoned after the 1882-83 divisions. No fewer than seventeen Brethren-related schools were established, several of which survived into the later 20th century: Juniata College (PA, 1876), *Bridgewater College (VA, 1889), *McPherson College (KS, 1887), the University of *La Verne (CA, 1891), *Manchester College (IN, 1895), and *Elizabethtown College (PA, 1900). These schools began as secondary level *academies offering a few college level courses with a focus on teacher education.

While all of these schools eventually offered Bible courses, they were not primarily *Bible colleges, but rather liberal arts institutions. The dream of a school for training church workers, pastors, and missionaries was realized by *A. C. Wieand and *E. B. Hoff in 1905 with the founding in Chicago of Bethany Bible School (*Bethany Theological Seminary). By that time the professional minister and church worker vocations, almost unthought of fifty years earlier, had become permanent features of the church's life. By the 1960s the plural, *free, nonsalaried ministry had been virtually replaced by the salaried pastor.

A related development was the *Sunday School movement, which also blossomed into full flower after the 1882-83 divisions (*Christian Education). Beginning with the Sunday School Advisory Board (1896) and its numerous successors, the denomination assumed the leadership for supplying literature and teacher training. Publications such as the *Brethren Teachers Quarterly (1899) and lessons based on the *International Sunday School Lessons began to appear. By the turn of the century most congregations operated a church school, usually before Sunday worship. Many also began to have *Daily Vacation Bible Schools, weekday schools, and other programs for youth. Attendance at Sunday schools increased dramatically after 1900 to reach a high of 168,503 in 1960.

Outdoor Christian education also began to have an impact on the denomination through summer *camping programs. The first of these is thought to have been held in Nebraska in 1916, although other "summer assemblies" were soon operating in Indiana, Idaho, and Pennsylvania. In the 1920s and 1930s most districts sought to initiate regular camping programs by developing permanent facilities. A typical week of intensive study, worship, and recreation, coupled with such visiting leaders as furloughed missionaries, created an environment where youth could be challenged to a life of Christian witness and service not possible in local church settings. In 1980 the twenty-four districts of the Church of the Brethren operated thirty-six camps.

ACCULTURATION: DRESS, ARCHITECTURE, WORSHIP. Certainly by 1910 acculturation brought about by evangelism and missions, publishing, and educational activities was irreversible. Brethren were too open, curious, and attracted to the society about them to be comfortable for long with a sectarian identity from the past. The strain produced by this tension was soon felt. The first major change was a shift in the practice of *nonconformity from an outward sign to an internal spirit or attitude. The "dress question" (church *discipline to enforce wearing of plain *dress) became one of the most widely discussed topics in the early 20th century. While plain dress had been an issue in the division of the 1880s, most members continued to wear the traditional garb. Although style varied according to geographic area, it generally included *beards, broadbrimmed *hats and *plain-cut coats for men; *bonnets, *prayer coverings, and *aprons for women.

As the denomination grew, the question of dress was raised repeatedly. Many argued that once freed from the restrictions of dress the Church of the Brethren would not only be more attractive to the secular world, but also that Brethren would be more free to address and minister to the needs of that world. In 1910 a regularly appointed Annual Meeting committee on dress reform brought back a carefully prepared report which called for strict uniformity of dress. Although the report was accepted, many thought it too general and another committee was appointed to prepare a supplementary policy statement. The conference asked that all debate on this issue in church papers cease until the special committee, chaired by *H. C. Early, brought its report to the 1911 conference at St.

Joseph, MO.

This committee's report, which was adopted, paved the way for the gradual discarding of distinctive dress. The St. Joseph statement strongly recommended the use of plain dress, especially for church officers, but failed to make it a test of church membership. The enforcement of dress thus became the option of local congregations, and as time passed fewer and fewer of them chose to require it as a condition of membership or a matter for church discipline. In 1980 only a handful of congregations in eastern Pennsylvania and Maryland continue to expect their members or officials to wear plain dress. Most Brethren, however, continue to affirm the value of modest and simple clothing (*simple life).

The change did not come about without the breaking of denominational unity. In 1926 the *Dunkard Brethren group, who continued the practice of distinctive dress and was opposed to other liberal trends, withdrew from the church. This movement centered around the periodical *Bible Monitor* (1922), published and edited by *B. E. Kesler. Kesler, a member of the 1910 dress committee, served as the first moderator of the Dunkard Brethren General Conference in 1927. This schism affected more than thirty congregations, primarily in Pennsylvania, Maryland, Indiana, and Ohio.

Brethren were changing not only their personal appearance but the style of their houses of worship as well. The typical *meetinghouse in 1880 was a simple frame building with twin doors — one entrance for the men, another for the women. The congregation was seated facing a long speakers' table which was not elevated or decorated. Indeed there were no particular symbols to designate the room as a meeting for worship. This style changed in the last quarter of the 19th century as Brethren began to copy church buildings of their *Baptist and (*United) Methodist neighbors. A typical "chapel" had a raised platform at one end of the house with a *pulpit squarely in the middle. A cross and other visual symbols were present, as well as a steeple (for a *bell) and possibly windows with colored glass panes. Pianos or reed organs soon appeared to accompany congregational singing. Permanent pews replaced portable benches which meant that the *love feast was often relegated to the basement.

As a new wave of church building began in the 1950s and 1960s, professional architects were employed to design "more beautiful" and "reverent" sanctuaries in traditional Protestant styles. Usually little attention was given to particular Brethren beliefs or practices, except for the installation of a heated baptistry. The center pulpit was frequently replaced by a divided chancel, with a lectern on one side and the pulpit on the other. At the center of the chancel was typically a communion table (commonly called an "altar") with a cross, Bible, and other elements of a worship center. The *love feast was now held in the "fellowship hall" of the educational wing, built to accommodate an expanding church school program. Reed organs were replaced with electronic or pipe organs, colored panes with more elaborate stained glass in windows.

If it may be said that the primary characteristic of modern Brethren church *architecture is variety, the same may be said of Brethren *worship. Obviously the changes in building design reflected what had happened to worship. Nineteenth-century Brethren worship had an air of spontaneity and informality as two or more ministers *preached on a common theme. Several *hymns and prayers were also part of the service. As time passed the preached word remained the focus of worship, but the service itself became more structured and planned, as evidenced by the move to salaried pastors and the publication of the first worship *manuals in 1882 and 1887. Twentieth-century manuals have included various liturgical helps and aids, as have various editions of *The Brethren Hymnal* (1925, 1951). Some congregations have moved to a more formal liturgy, following some seasons of the church year, and accompanied by more sophisticated choral music. Other congregations retained the informality and closeness of former years.

MILITARY SERVICE. While shifts in dress, architecture, and worship were accompanied by tension, they occurred slowly. When the USA entered *World War I in 1917 Brethren were confronted with an unforeseen problem of immense importance for which they were unprepared. The result was a redefinition of the historic doctrine of *nonresistance. The position of Brethren in previous wars had been clear. Members must obey the law and pay special war related *taxes (although resisters were also supported); they might pay a *commutation fee or even on occasion hire a *substitute to avoid service; but they could not join the armed forces, even if drafted. In 1917-18 the reaction was different. In 1917 Gov. Brumbaugh chose state duties over Brethren peace principles and called the state militia of Pennsylvania to active duty. Other Brethren supported the war, at least minimally, by suppressing their German heritage, buying war bonds, and working in *defense industries. Some even willingly entered the armed forces.

The 1917 conscription law provided that those opposed to war on religious grounds could serve as noncombatants, but it took the administration nearly a year to decide which branches of service should be declared noncombatant. Those corps so designated — engineering, quartermaster, medical — were unacceptable to many Brethren. In the meantime young Brethren men were being drafted without guidance from the church on how far they could cooperate with the military. Some were treated harshly in the camps.

In an attempt to clarify the church's position on war and military service, church leaders called a special delegated conference in January, 1918, at Goshen, IN. Among other provisions, the *"Goshen Statement" urged

Brethren not to enlist and not to wear the military uniform. When this advice (in printed form) reached Washington, DC, the War Department threatened criminal prosecution of church officials on charges of sedition. The statement was withdrawn, thus avoiding possible trial and imprisonment, but at the cost of weakening the Brethren *peace witness. World War I ended without any set policy and with most drafted Brethren in uniform accepting some form of noncombatant service.

The frustration of some young men in dealing with issues of the draft and military service caused a few to dedicate their lives to peace work. Two of the most widely known and respected were *M. R. Zigler and *Dan West. Zigler had worked with the YMCA during the war. He became home missions secretary for the General Mission Board in 1919 and later served in several major administrative and leadership roles, including significant *ecumenical involvement. West, who served in the army, attempted to renew peace work in the 1930s through *relief work and a movement called *"One Hundred Dunkers for Peace." Following the *Spanish Civil War he was the founder of the *Heifer Project. In 1935 Annual Conference flatly asserted that "all war is sin," a statement which became the basis for later peace activities.

During the 1930s Brethren leaders also began to cooperate closely with representatives of the *Society of Friends (Quakers) and *Mennonites—the *historic peace churches—in an effort to avoid the mistakes of World War I. These churches were agreed that no form of military service, including noncombatant service, was acceptable to *conscientious objectors (COs). As the United States drifted toward war in 1940 and another conscription act was being written, representatives of the historic peace churches and the military agreed that COs, when drafted, should not be assigned to army camps, but be placed in alternative work camps "under civilian direction."

This led to the organization of *Civilian Public Service (CPS) in which various government agencies took responsibility for work projects while church agencies funded the program and directed camp life. The *Brethren Service Committee (later Brethren Service Commission), organized in 1939, was restructured in 1941 and given responsibility for operating such camps. Eventually the BSC operated fourteen camps between 1941 and 1947 at a cost of over two million dollars. Brethren CPS men were also released from *base camps to perform *emergency farm labor, to work in *mental hospitals, to serve as forest *fire fighters and to volunteer as subjects of medical experiments. Public opinion on these programs of alternate service was largely favorable. The *National Service Board for Religious Objectors (*National Interreligious Service Board for Conscientious Objectors) was set up in 1941 to serve as a liaison between the BSC and other church agencies operating CPS projects and the Selective Service System.

Some 1,350 Church of the Brethren men served in CPS during *World War II. This was the first war in which more than half of all young Brethren men either volunteered for or served as combatants in the armed forces when drafted. During the 1950s and 1960s the church continued to present a *peace witness but somehow the spirit had changed. Although Cold War political issues were sometime intense, there seemed to be greater ease in dealing with Selective Service. The church knew that it could provide an alternative to military duty, and it had leaders who knew how to work with the government.

Consequently, alternative service was also available to COs during the *Korean and *Vietnam wars. *Brethren Volunteer Service, created in 1948 largely from the pressure of older youth at Annual Conference and the threat of a peacetime draft, replaced CPS. Work assignments were considerably more flexible than during World War II and almost totally under church supervision. Still, only a minority of the members considered themselves Christian "pacifists." The Vietnam conflict was particularly trying for the church. For one thing, the church was slow to condemn increased US military activity in Vietnam during the mid-1960s. As the country became divided, so did the church and emotions were tense when, in 1970, one young Brethren protester publically burned his draft card at Annual Conference. The death of *Ted Studebaker while doing alternative service in Vietnam in 1971 seemed to indicate the futility and senselessness of the war. A tiny minority chose non-cooperation and refused both alternative service and military duty when drafted.

In response to the Vietnam war, some Brethren, primarily college age youth, banded together in such organizations as the Brethren Action Movement (BAM) and in Pennyslvania, the *Brethren Peace Fellowship (BPF). BAM, more of a movement than an organization, called the church to social responsibility, especially in peace education. Small BAM groups formed in various locations — some interested keenly in living in intentional communities, others in New Left politics. Although BAM formally disbanded in 1975 certain key individuals, such as Art Gish and Dale Aukerman, have continued to articulate these concerns. A more recent organization, the *On Earth Peace assembly, was inspired and convened by M. R. Zigler in 1974 to combat the increased militarization of society.

In 1979-80 the issue for many shifted to whether or not to register for a possible future draft. Enten Eller, a Bridgewater College student, in a widely publicized trial, was the first to be convicted for nonregistration (1982).

RELATION TO THE STATE, BRETHREN SERVICE. The problem of involvement with the military was reflected in the wider issue of Brethren *church-state relations in the

20th century. The suspicion, distrust, and separatism which characterized Brethren in the 19th century were gone. An early expression of this change was Annual Conference support for *prohibition. Previous actions against traffic in or use of *alcoholic beverages had been directed at members, with caution against participation in the wider *temperance movement. In 1918, however, delegates pledged their "hearty support" for passage of the 18th Amendment to the US Constitution.

Clearly by the end of World War I most Brethren voted in political *elections. Although no statistics are available, they tended to support the Republican Party. In the 1930s the economic depression and New Deal programs brought some realignment of political party preference, although certain caution remained into the 1940s regarding *labor union membership and activities. In more recent years Brethren have publically supported candidates concerned about peace issues, civil rights, and *social welfare programs.

Three very different Brethren in the post-World War II period illustrate how fully church members had become involved with government and improvement of the social order. They were *Andrew W. Cordier, *Kermit Eby, and *Ralph E. Smeltzer. Cordier, a Manchester College history professor, became a senior official in the Department of State, undersecretary to two secretary-generals of the *United Nations, and president of Columbia U. Eby, who came from an Indiana farm background, was active in the Congress of Industrial Organization in Michigan and served as its national education director in the 1940s. Later a professor at the U. of Chicago, he was an articulate advocate of Brethren heritage and liberal social concerns. Although not as well known, Smeltzer had a remarkable career as a churchman concerned for others. From 1942, when he assisted the *American Friends Service Committee in relocating displaced *Japanese-Americans, to 1964, as a mediator in racially torn Selma,

AL, to his untimely death in 1976, Smeltzer was an effective witness for social justice.

Closely related to the task of cooperating with and witnessing to government were efforts in international *relief. Like foreign missions, such projects began modestly but dramatically increased as Brethren came to see the need to help alleviate suffering regardless of who the victims were, where they lived, or what their religious belief was. In 1917 Annual Conference authorized relief aid to *Armenians, and by 1921 over $260,000 had been raised.

In the 1930s the Japanese invasion of China and the Spanish Civil War brought forth Brethren involvement in relief efforts, both through funds and voluntary service. At the conclusion of World War II the Brethren Service Committee shifted from CPS administration back to its original purpose and launched a major relief effort in many countries in Europe and around the globe. Such projects as *work camps, *student exchanges, distribution of *material aid, (food, medicine, and clothing), and agricultural programs, were initiated. In *Austria activities centered on working with *displaced persons and the *Volksdeutsche, who were not eligible for state assisted relief programs. In *Poland, agricultural exchanges begun in 1947 had to be suspended because of Cold War tensions but were later resumed. BSC also had projects in West *Germany, *Greece, *Spain, *Belgium, and *Italy, as well as the Far East.

Much of this work was guided by M. R. Zigler who was the executive director of BSC until 1948 and then served as director of Brethren Service in Europe with headquarters in Geneva, Switzerland.

The former *Blue Ridge College campus at *New Windsor, MD, was purchased in 1944 and converted into a depot for relief aid collections, and site of volunteer training. It later became a center for *Church World Service, the relief and service agency of the *National Council of Churches. It is fair to say that Brethren participation in these activities, which seemed so much more positive than the "no" of the church to military duty, replaced foreign missions as the most prominent work of the denomination.

As Europe recovered in the late 1950s and 1960s, there was less demand for service projects in Europe. Still, in 1966, after twenty-five years of operation, the BSC had 430 persons placed in 15 foreign countries. After the *World Ministries Commission assumed the work of Brethren Service in 1968, there was a shift from distribution of food and clothing to programs of economic and social development in Asia, Africa, and Latin America.

Many Brethren Service projects won international recognition; some took more permanent form with former volunteers serving in staff positions. A partial list includes *Heifer Project, *International Christian Youth Exchange (ICYE), *Sales Exchange for Refugee Rehabilitation Vocations (SERRV), *Christian Rural Overseas Program (CROP), and *International Voluntary Service (IVS), a forerunner of the *Peace Corps.

THEOLOGICAL STABILITY. The changes in Brethren life which took place in the first half of the 20th century were accompanied by a search for theological stability. While the church may have discovered its uniqueness in serving the world, it was less sure of its own identity. The roots of the Brethren movement were in *Anabaptism and *Pietism. Yet neither of these seemed very dynamic in 1900˙ and both would have been almost completely rejected by many. A host of denominational leaders in the interwar years obtained theological and higher education at such graduate schools as the U. of Chicago, Yale U., Vanderbilt U. and Columbia U. Some, such as *D. W. Kurtz, even studied in Europe. They were informed on the latest issues of biblical scholarship and interpretation, thus moving the church away from the simple literalism characteristic of the 19th century. Many also adopted *social gospel theology and envisioned a Brethren church engaged in social service. This group dominated national leadership and was committed to ecumenical dialog (*ecumenism) and the conciliar movement. Although the first attempt at this type of activity (participation in the *Interchurch World Movement) failed, the Church of the Brethren cooperated in international relief projects, joined the Federal (*National Council of Churches) in 1941, and became a charter member of the *World Council of Churches in 1948.

After the Dunkard Brethren withdrew in 1926, new conservative pressures were felt in the Church of the Brethren. More traditional Brethren simply wished the church to be less involved with mainstream Protestantism. Others were influenced by a resurgence of *Fundamentalism. One of the first tests of fundamentalist strength was felt in the M. Pennsylvania district. Under the leadership of *C. C. Ellis, Juniata College established a conservative *school of theology. A potential division was defused when Annual Meeting assumed control of Bethany Bible School in 1925 and the Juniata school closed.

Membership of the denomination in both the National and World Council of Churches has been a continuing sore point for some conservative Brethren. Although a majority of Annual Conference delegates have consistently supported membership in these bodies, a minority has repeatedly called for a reconsideration of this decision. Objections have ranged from opposition to cooperation in any ecumenical venture for fear of creating an apostate world church, to charges of *Modernism, *Liberalism, and, more recently, Marxism, as well as support for unpopular political, economic, and justice issues by council leadership.

In the 1940s two M. Pennsylvania congregations (Lewistown and Altoona, 28th St.) suffered schisms over Fundamentalism. Four small Carolina congregations left in the 1960s over similar issues (*Fundamental Brethren Churches). Occasionally Church of the Brethren congregations have been seriously divided when pastors or other leaders became more comfortable with Grace Brethren theology. This has happened to congregations in Florida, Ohio, Michigan, Pennsylvania, and elsewhere. There has also been some shifting of membership between denominations over these issues.

Although not Fundamentalists, conservatives in the 1950s and following found a voice through the organization of the *Brethren Revival Fellowship (BRF) in 1959. The BRF holds that a sectarian model is still valid for Brethren and places heavy emphasis on biblical authority, evangelism, anabaptist doctrine, and traditional Brethren practices. This group has been sharply critical of alleged Liberalism and Modernism in denominational programs and *Sunday school curricula and of denominational participation in the ecumenical movement. The strength of this group is primarily in Pennsylvania, although BRF literature can be found in numerous congregations across the country.

The crucial test of Brethren ecumenicity came in 1966 with the *Consultation on Church Union (COCU). This consultation was created in 1962 in an effort to merge the major Protestant groups to form a church that would be "truly reformed, truly Catholic, and truly evangelical." While Brethren representatives attended early meetings as observers, an invitation was extended in 1965 to become full members. This became a highly emotional issue as debate took place in local churches, districts, church periodicals, and other settings on what membership in COCU might mean. Some viewed the merger as necessary for any meaningful witness to the state and the world. Others felt that the Brethren would be swallowed up in a church of possibly twenty to thirty million members, thus losing Brethen beliefs and distinctive New Testament practices. At the tension-filled 1966 Annual Conference at

Louisville, KY, delegates decisively voted against full membership, yet reaffirmed their commitment to cooperative and conciliar ecumenical relationships. In 1968 Conference voted not to reopen the COCU question.

Brethren ecumenical relations were also illustrated by the *New Call to Peacemaking movement, a grass-roots, renewal effort by Brethren, Friends, and Mennonites to oppose militarism and the nuclear arms race in the 1970s and 1980s. Other such activities include conversations with the *American Baptist Churches USA which fell short of merger but led to a covenant of association in 1973. This cooperation is evident in part by cooperation between Bethany Theological Seminary and Northern Baptist Seminary and in six congregations (1980) which are affiliated with both denominations. Perhaps the most unusual ecumenical dialog took place in the late 1960s and early 1970s with the *Russian Orthodox Church. In 1967 Metropolitan *Nikodim visited local congregations, church-related colleges, Bethany Theological Seminary, and denominational offices, usually accompanied by the protests of Fundamentalists. Brethren delegations also visited *Russian Orthodox centers in the USSR.

Theological stability has been tested by the changing status and increasing importance of *women in the life of the church. This role had clearly begun to change by 1910, when sisters began to break bread at love feast, rather than having a male elder hand it to them (*Julia A. Gilbert). Although gifted women had served as preachers for several decades previously, it was not until 1922 that they were formally eligible for *licensing. *Ordination was not permitted until 1958. With the emergence of the feminist movement in the 1960s and 1970s, Brethren women formed the *Womaen's Caucus group in 1973. This organization has been successful in securing a national staff position for *"person awareness" and calling the church to sensitivity in using inclusive language in its publications.

A stirring of quite different character has been the *charismatic movement which has grown significantly since 1960 in almost every major denomination. Several Church of the Brethren leaders, including Pittsburgh pastor Russell Bixler and former missionaries *Chalmer and Mary Faw, experienced a renewing and rededication of the work of the *Holy Spirit in their lives and ministry. An informal steering committee has planned Annual Conference activities and, since 1974, annual Holy Spirit conferences. While the charismatic renewal movement has seriously divided some congregations, others have experienced a richer *spiritual life.

Institutionally the Brethren have worked at renewal through such programs as *Mission Twelve and *Mission One. The Mission Twelve plan, created in 1962, used small group retreat settings where members from local congregations could explore interpersonal communication and Christian community. The Mission One emphasis in the late 1960s was largely unstructured but encouraged Brethren to turn to the world around them in mission. Church publications highlighted the theme of "God Loved the World So. . ." but local response was mixed. One result, however, was the creation of the Fund for the Americas in 1969 (*SHARE) to raise monies for minority group self-help projects. There was heightened concern during this period for American *minorities seeking identity and liberation. The church, through Annual Conference statements and resolutions and through district and local outreach, has supported blacks, Hispanics, native Americans, and white *Appalachians.

This activity suggests that the Church of the Brethren has frequently spoken with a more distinct voice on "outside concerns" than the inner life. This issue as well as a search for theological stability resulted in two unique series of conferences. The first of these, the so-called *Puidoux Conferences took place in Europe between 1955 and 1962 with representatives from the state churches of West Germany, the Mennonites, Quakers, and Brethren. Although not widely publicized, the result was a new appreciation by Brethren of the *Believers' Church heritage. A second series of gatherings, *theological study conferences, were called to help clarify various theological questions. The first, in 1960, centered on the "Nature and Function of the Church." The second, in 1964, focused on the meaning of church membership. A third conference in 1969 dealt with "Faithfulness in Change" and affirmed the basic unity of the church in the midst of diversity. The fourth in this series, a "Biblical/Theological Quest" in 1981 was open to wider participation in order to help the church become more theologically articulate. All of these conferences included position papers, worship and study, and intensive discussion.

CHURCH STRUCTURE. The years since World War II have seen two complete reorganizations of denominational life. With the publishing house and General Mission Board located in Elgin, IL, nw. of Chicago, in 1900, it was only natural that national staff and bureaucracy evolved here (popularly referred to as "Elgin") to administer the denomination's many programs and to implement Annual Conference decisions (*General Offices). The 1920s and 1930s saw a multiplication of boards and committees, all reporting to Annual Conference, many needing full-time staff members, but each independent of the other. As boards took on more responsibilities, were reorganized, merged, and shifted programs, areas of authority seemed to conflict as they competed with one another for tight funds. The three most powerful of these were the General Mission Board, the Brethren Publishing House (*Brethren Press), and the *Board of Christian Education.

By the mid 1940s there was enough dissatisfaction with this arrangement to create a more unified system of organization. In 1946 a select committee of fifteen developed a plan of organization which was given conference approval the following year. This created a General Brotherhood Board of twenty-five members with five commissions that incorporated the previously independent boards and committees. *Raymond R. Peters was the first executive secretary, followed in 1952 by *Norman J. Baugher. Also, geographic *regions (each encompassing several districts) originally shaped to reflect the constituencies of the church-related colleges, were created with their own staffs and programs. Districts within these regions by this time had employed field secretaries to assist with pastoral *placement and built and operated *retirement homes, *orphanages, and camps. Although there were now four levels of *polity (congregation, district, region, and denomination), business for Annual Conference bypassed the regional structure.

This plan lasted until 1968, when another major reorganization took place. The regional structure had not worked well and was dissolved. The new *General Board was divided into three commissions — World Ministries, *Parish Ministries, and *General Services — each led by an associate general secretary, with overall responsibility given to a general secretary. *S. Loren Bowman served as the first general secretary until his retirement in 1978; he was followed by Robert W. Neff.

Changes in structure were accompanied by changes in physical location. The old general offices and publishing house located on S. State St., were moved to a modern facility on the northern outskirts of Elgin in 1959. Four years later Bethany Biblical Seminary abandoned its inner-city Chicago location to move to a spacious suburban campus at Oak Brook. The proximity of denominational offices and seminary created a kind of "Elgin-Bethany" complex of leadership, with many members blurring the distinction between the two institutions. A new *Bethany (Brethren) Hospital was under construction in 1983.

In congregational life the role of the salaried pastor in worship and program has continued to increase in importance. Seminary training is normally a prerequisite for ordination and pastoral service. Consequently, the role of *elders in a supervisory capacity over congregations was diminished. After several studies, this historic office was terminated in 1967, although those previously ordained as elders remained in office for life. In 1958 congregations were given permission by Annual Conference to accept members of other denominations without *baptism or rebaptism in the Brethren manner. The idea of a unified denominational budget, introduced with the reorganization of 1946, gained gradual acceptance, although in the 1980s this showed signs of reversing as more and more special offerings compete for local funds. Brethren *polity thus remains a combination of congregational and presbyterian forms, with much lee way for development of local programs.

The late 1960s brought a sharp fall in the Church of the Brethren membership in the USA, which reached a peak in 1963 of 202,257 but by 1980 stood at 170,839. Renewed interest in evangelism was evidenced by participation in the "Key '73" program and a 1974 conference on evangelism in Dayton, OH. There has also been keen interest in the church growth movement (*church extension) and other methods of home missions. There are signs in the early 1980s that efforts to increase church membership and plant new congregations may replace peace and service activities as the single most important priority of the denomination.

In the hundred years between 1883 and 1983 the Church of the Brethren has come through a period of remarkable change. In that process the most obvious thing that the church lost was a sense of community and sectarian identity. Yet it gained, in turn, visions for world missions and later world service that had an impact far beyond what might be expected of a small denomination.

Dunkard Brethren (DB). This branch of the Brethren originated in 1926 in response to various developments within the Church of the Brethren in the late 19th and early 20th centuries. Publications and improved organization had united the denomination, and in the period around 1910 the Church of the Brethren experienced a revival and reconsecration. The church had a tremendous missionary zeal, spreading to India, China, and Nigeria. The General Sunday School Board (1911) and the General Educational Board (1908) replaced ad hoc committees (Sunday School Advisory Committee, School Visiting Committees) and joined the *publishing and missions programs to lay the foundation of a denominational structure.

What happened after this was seen in different light by various observers. A series of events led to a division and the formation of the Dunkard Brethren in 1926. *John S. Flory (CB), in *Flashlights from History* (1932), called the new organization another "mistake." He felt its leaders were looking backward instead of toward the future and that they were clinging to the church as a "fixed institution." "These good people have nothing to offer the world that the church from which they withdrew does not have," he stated. "They forget that the church is to serve the world. Although the world is constantly changing, the church must continue to do its work as it did in the 'good old times' of long ago. When the church adapts its methods of work to meet changed conditions, they raise the cry of apostasy, departure from the faith."

The Dunkard Brethren understanding of the purpose of the church was probably the real cause of the separation. Flory considered the purpose of the church to be service to the world. Dunkard Brethren believed that the church should hold up a standard to the world. There is a distinct difference here. Serving the world leads to compromise, believers lose ground, and in the end they lose that for which they compromised. As a "dissenting" group, Dunkard Brethren felt the standard was being lowered.

The matter of plain *dress and fashion conformity illustrated this lowered standard. The 1911 Annual Meeting dress decision presented clear guidelines for simplicity and decency. For the brethren the *plain coat with a standing collar was advised. For the sisters, garments free from ornaments, and plain *bonnets and hoods were recommended. This dress decision was not a new idea, but rather a writing down of the general principles that guided the church throughout its history. Yet by 1926 *neckties and stylish hats were being worn in the Church of the Brethren. The fashionable *hairstyles of the time were also appearing in the churches.

*Divorce also was being accepted by the church. The previous stance of the brotherhood was to hold that fornication was the only scriptural grounds for divorce and that the divorced person should not remarry. The Church of the Brethren also changed its course when its members started joining lodges. Affiliation with *secret societies had previously been rejected as being unscriptural.

An emphasis on the *youth of the church grew in the decade before the division. An all-out effort was made to keep the youth in the church (*Committee on Saving Our Children to the Church). This youth movement was also advanced by the beginnings of the church *camping programs. Such activities tended to isolate the youth from the older generation; instead of uniting the two, it caused a larger gap. It limited the interaction and the teaching that was needed in a body of true believers. Also in holding forth entertainment rather than truth as the attracting force it compromised with the main aim of the church.

Increasing weight was placed on *education also as the initial Brethren-related schools, primarily *academies and *Normal schools, developed into four-year liberal arts colleges. Some of the Brethren felt the emphasis had switched from practical knowledge and basic literacy to a desire for knowledge for its own sake. They felt that secular education was good as long as it was secondary to or complementary to *Christian education. These dissenting Brethren even stated their assent to secular education in the minutes of reorganization in 1926. Yet they felt that form of education supported by the church was leading the church away from valuable principles and causing the line between the church and the world to become hazy.

Hand-in-hand with this came the *salaried minister. Perhaps to some this seems the inevitable outcome of an educated ministry. However the presence of salaried ministers initiated a change in roles within the congregation. Where formerly the congregation was led by a group of elders or ministers working together with *lay members, now the church was led by a single person. The congregation-centered church shifted towards a pastor-centered one. Duties of lay members and the deacons and decisions formerly made by the congregation were placed into the pastor's hands. Some of the Brethren resisted this change because they saw it as deviating from the example set by the New Testament church.

These deviations from former ways did not happen without protest. Concerned congregations sent queries and petitions to the general conferences "designed to 'bring back' the church to its former ways of doing things." Their attempts failed. *B. E. Kesler became a leader of this body of dissatisfied members. Kesler was an elder in the Church of the Brethren in Missouri. He was known for his clarity and wit in public *debate. In 1923 he began to publish a paper at Poplar Bluff, MO, called *The Bible Monitor. Its purpose was to give this small core of believers a "means to counteract the worldward drift of the church" and to inform the general body of this drift. This attempt to bring reform was misunderstood and resulted in the ostracization of those concerned. Matters came to a climax when Elder Kesler, sent to Annual Conference (1923) by his congregation, was refused a seat by the credentials committee at the Annual Conference. The NW. Ohio district passed a decision that prohibited ministers who supported the *Monitor* from preaching in the churches of the district.

The first meeting of the "*Monitor* family," that is, those advocating reform, was held at Denton, MD, on Sept. 12, 1923. Its purpose was to decide the course for the future. It was recorded that "the Spirit of the meeting was excellent and that the Holy Spirit was present." A brother attending the meeting observed, "Much good came from the little meeting held in Denton, MD, Sept. 12. May the influence going out from it cause our brethren to take heed to their ways and lead them to seek the old paths of truth and righteousness."

A second meeting was held at *Uniontown, PA, on June 5-6, 1924. The Brethren pushed for a new vigor in the "*Bible Monitor* Movement." Another meeting for unity and understanding gathered at Wauseon, OH, June 4-5, 1925. At various other meetings throughout the brotherhood, such as the two meetings held in Henry Kegerreis's barn near Jonestown, Lebanon Co., PA, Brethren gathered to discuss the church's situation and the *Monitor* family's position. With an increasing number of followers and a decreasing ability to work within the existing body, the *Monitor* movement began to focus on the possibility of starting a new Brethren fellowship.

June 23, 1926, brought another meeting into session at Plevna, IN. This time a decision was deemed necessary. On June 24 the Brethren decided that they, "as a part of the loyal and faithful of the present Church of the Brethren see no other remedy for relief than to obey the gospel, and to declare ourselves independent, and to reorganize, and to reestablish the true faith of the gospel amongst us." The movement became the Dunkard Brethren Church.

The Brethren adopted a *"Declaration of Principles" to guide the new body. In setting up their polity they returned to the dress decision of 1911, with only minor changes. The meeting also adopted a series of doctrinal statements, asserting that the Dunkard Brethren creed is the New Testament (*noncreedalism). They believe that the Bible is the inspired word of God. (The Authorized [King James] version is used in church services.) The Godhead is one, consisting of the Father, the Son (the promised Messiah, Redeemer, and Savior of the world) and the *Holy Spirit. Man fell from his state of purity by voluntary sin; through faith, *repentance, *confession, and *baptism, man can be redeemed by the atonement of our Savior. Baptism by trine immersion for the remission of sins prepares man for the new birth; by which the volition, affections, and desires are changed from the love of things fleshly to the love of things spiritual and heavenly. Until 1946 new members (with certain exceptions for former Old German Baptist Brethren) were *rebaptized; in 1980 trine immersion administered by Christian groups "similar" to the Dunkard Brethren is considered valid.

Dunkard Brethren practice the following New Testament *ordinances: the holy *kiss, the traditional Brethren *love feast (including *feetwashing and unleavened bread and unfermented cup [*grape juice]). The use of *tobacco, intoxicating beverages (*alcohol), and *television is forbidden. Taking part in politics and learning the art of war is against the *nonresistant teaching of the New Testament. Participation in games, plays, performances, secret societies, and *labor unions which are manifestly evil is contrary to the gospel and a pure heart. Wearing of hats by Christian women and of neckties, gold ornaments, rings, bracelets, and other *jewelry by either sex is a token of a proud heart. Honesty, simplicity, and modesty in dress and manners have been the teaching of the Dunkard Brethren since their beginning. The hair should be worn in a plain and sanitary manner; women are expected to wear the plain white *cap, at least in time of prayer and prophesying. Long hair worn by men and short hair worn by women are forbidden. *Musical instruments are forbidden in the church. Members do not swear or subscribe to the civil *oath; they do not go to *law without the permission of the church. Life *insurance is discouraged and divorce is forbidden. Matthew 18:10-22 is used to adjust differences in the church. The church has supremacy over the individual and all problems are solved by local, district, and general conferences.

In the 1980s the aim of the Dunkard Brethren remains "to be more sanctified, more righteous, more holy, and more perfect through faith and obedience." In nearly fifty years of existence, the Dunkard Brethren polity booklet has changed only slightly, although practice varies somewhat. Dunkard Brethren have this to offer the world: they remain a body with the goal of fulfilling God's purpose for them. Dunkard Brethren understand their purpose, as the "light of the world," to be that of pointing to the truth which God reveals in the Bible. They search the Scriptures and attempt to apply them to their lives. They advocate quiet living and *humility before God and man.

After 50 years, the Dunkard Brethren numbered ca. 1,035 members in 26 congregations (1980). They have no official headquarters, although this was an item under study in the mid-1970s. The congregations are organized into four districts under the authority of the General Conference. The *Dunkard Brethren Church Polity* booklet defines the principles, practices, and doctrines of the church. The *Dunkard Brethren Church Manual* (1971) provides administrative information.

The local congregations are small democracies in themselves. Any member over twelve has voting rights. The decisions are final for any local matter. A presiding elder chosen by the congregation from the elders' body is in charge of the local church *council meetings. The council meets quarterly or on specific occasions as the need arises. All business discussed at the council meeting first passes the official body, a group composed of the *deacons, *elders, and ministers.

The eldership is the highest office of the church. Elders are chosen from among the ministers in the congregations where they hold their membership. The elders of the district have the authority to ordain other elders, but the ordination is based on the private votes of the membership. "All elders present at General Conference, and who [sic] constitute Standing Committee, have the oversight of the Brotherhood at large. They, with the ministers and deacons present, compose General Conference; they preside in district conferences and in local church councils, ordain other elders, anoint the sick, solemnize marriages, officiate at communion services, preach the gospel, baptize and see that the principles and usages of the church are respected and carried out in the lives of the membership, they themselves being examples to the flock in obedience and holiness of life."

Ministers and *deacons are also elected by the congregation. The duties of a minister are preaching, baptizing, assisting elders in *anointing, solemnizing *marriages, and officiating at communion services. Deacons are chosen to look after the financial and temporal needs of the church. "They serve at communion, visit the sick, care for the *poor, assist in the ministry, investigate troubles, pay the Church Visit [*deacons' visit], and may in extreme cases administer baptism and assist in anointing."

District meetings are held annually, rotating from congregation to congregation throughout the district. The

business matters dealt with have been previously for-
warded to the district meeting from local churches. These
may be dealt with at the district meeting or passed on to
the General Conference.

Three delegates from each congregation gather to
form the voting body of the district. These delegates are
chosen by vote of the congregations. The only qualifica-
tion required is they must be members who follow the
*order of the church.

General Conference has the final authority on the
matters brought before it. Delegates are any elder,
minister, or deacon who has been before the Credentials
Committee and has been passed. Business comes to the
General Conference through one of the four districts.
Those bringing the matter before the Conference have the
privilege of explanation. If no objections are offered, the
paper is passed. A simple majority vote is required if objections are raised; doctrinal questions require a two-
thirds majority vote.

Dunkard Brethren support the *Torreon Navajo Mission in New Mexico. Other organized mission points are at
Elkins, VA; Hart, MI; Clearville, PA; in several additional
locations ministers are sent in regularly to preach to scattered
members. The congregations separately support other local
or worldwide missionary or relief effort not organized by the
church. They are also responsible for taking care of the needs
of their own members.

Fellowship of Grace Brethren Churches (FGBC), the larger group of congregations that developed from the *Progressive Brethren movement of the last half of the 19th century. With a membership of 42,023 in the USA (1981), the 284 Grace Brethren congregations are most heavily concentrated in California, Ohio, and Pennsylvania. These churches are *fundamentalist, or evangelical, in character, with a heavy emphasis on *missions and sharing the gospel ("soul winning"). Much of a member's life is spent in a subculture of frequent church attendance and rigorous adherence to separation from the world, as perceived by 20th-century American Evangelicalism. Each congregation is self-governing and operates through an elected official board. National concerns are reflected by local organizations that support missions, *Christian education, *youth work, and other activities. The minister usually has an authoritative role in these congregations, often serving as moderator of the official board and of the congregational meetings.

The congregations are organized into nineteen districts, each of which holds an annual conference. These are generally operated along the same lines as the National Conference and provide for the ordination and discipline of ministers, women's groups, district missions, and youth activities.

The National Conference of the Fellowship of Grace Brethren Churches meets each summer, usually at *Winona Lake, IN, although on occasion the conference is held in other locations, such as Florida (1979) and California (1982). This assembly conducts church business, studies the Bible, and listens to reports from committees and affiliated organizations. Delegates to the conference include ordained ministers, and representatives from the local congregations and from the district conferences. These delegates elect the officers and the committees of the fellowship. Committees include those on membership, resolutions, hospitality, auditing, music, publicity, evangelism, Christian education, ministry, nominations, and sanctity of life. There are also cooperating organizations, such as the Foreign Missionary Society of the Grace Brethren Church, the Brethren Home Missions Council, Grace Theological Seminary and Grace College (*Grace Schools), the Brethren Missionary Herald Co., the National Fellowship of Grace Brethren Ministers, the Women's Missionary Council, the National Fellowship of Grace Brethren Men and Boys, and Brethren Retirement Homes, Inc.

DIVISION. The FGBC developed from struggles within the Progressive Brethren during the 1920s and 1930s. To those who formed the core of the early Grace Brethren it seemed that *liberalism was gaining ground in the denominational center at *Ashland College. They were upset by such individuals as *J. L. Gillin, president of the institution from 1907 to 1911, who proposed in his moderator's address at the general conference that "religious experience" be substituted for an "infallible Bible, as the true basis for Christian authority." Such statements led to the formulation of the "*Message of the Brethren Ministry" by a group that included *Alva J. McClain. This statement, adopted by the National Ministerial Association in 1921, became the rallying point for conservative forces within the church.

Another move made to strengthen the role of the fundamentalists within the church was the organization of a graduate school of theology in 1930 under the leadership of McClain. Because of economic difficulties it was housed on the same campus as Ashland College. Despite the success of the new foundation in training men for the ministry, friction arose between it and the college. In 1937 this hostility led to the dismissal of Dean McClain and *Herman A. Hoyt, two of the seminary's most popular professors. In protest most of the seminary students left, and in an effort to save them for the Brethren Church, Grace Theological Seminary was organized.

Two years later the existence of a separate seminary helped to cause division in the church. The exclusion of many delegates to the General Conference of 1939 at Winona Lake, led to a walkout of all those who represented churches that supported Grace Theological Seminary. They met in a nearby building and organized the National Brethren Bible Conference under the presidency of Herman A. Hoyt. This group helped to form the National Fellowship of Brethren Church (NFBC), which met in 1940. (In 1976 the official name was changed to Fellowship of Grace Brethren Churches.) It claimed to be the 51st annual meeting of the church to underscore the continuity with Brethren ideals. One of the early moderators of the group, *Louis S. Bauman, discussed the basis for the belief that the Grace Brethren were preserving Brethrenism in his 1942 address to the national conference. He found many similarities between the problems encountered in the 1930s by the Grace group and those faced by the Progressives in the 1880s. These boiled down to two major difficulties; one was the stuggle to maintain congregational church polity against those who wished to enforce ecclesiastical rules and laws and the other was the fight to keep the Word of God in the central place in the church's life. He stressed that: "A Brethren Church is a church with a certain well-defined faith and practice, proclaimed to the world since the days of Alexander Mack, over 200 years ago, and reaffirmed by our church fathers in 1883, and is a church rigidly con-

gregational in its form of government. Therefore, if a
Brethren Church ceases to be congregational in its form
of government, it, of it own volition, departs from the
well-defined practice of the Brethren Church, and by that
act automatically ceases to be a Brethren Church. It has
ex-communicated itself, whether it realizes it or not."
Bauman also believed that "the real Brethren faith (is) ab-
solute faith in the Holy Scriptures, and all that they contain, as being the sole rule for the faith and practice of any
and all born-again children of God."

Following the division in the church the differences
between the Ashland Brethren and the Grace Brethren
were intensified by a series of lawsuits involving church
property and bequests. In each of these cases the Ashland
group began the litigation. Following the scriptural
teaching of I Cor. 6:1-8, as interpreted by the Brethren
from the earliest days of the church, Grace supporters
have never initiated legal action. Faced with court action,
the Grace group has cited the example of Paul's appeal to
Caesar to justify defending itself.

These suits involved the First Brethren Church of
Dayton, OH (1940); the First Brethren Church of Peru,
IN (1943); the Brethren Church of Meyersdale, PA
(1947); and the Leon Brethren Church of Leon, IA
(1956). In addition there were lawsuits involving money
willed to some of the affiliated boards of the church. In
defending themselves the Grace Brethren argued that they
were congregationally governed and could not be forced
to support Ashland College or any of the central activities
of the Brethren. The Ashland group maintained that most
members of these churches were no longer affiliated with
the general conference; that they no longer supported the
college and other church ministries; and that they had
"departed in certain particulars from the fundamental
faith of the Brethren" by teaching salvation by faith
alone, the eternal security of the believer, and that baptism is not essential to salvation." *Homer A. Kent, Sr.,

the leading historian of the Grace movement, summed up the sad results of this litigation: "Statistics . . . do not favor either the Ashland or Grace group to any appreciable extent. . . [T]he Ashland group won the cases involving the Peru and Meyersdale churches, while the Grace constituency won the cases involving the Dayton and Leon churches. The Grace group also came off the victor in the William Johansen case involving a bequest. The gains on either side probably have not made up for the losses incurred by dragging our denominational differences into worldly courts."

FOREIGN AND HOME MISSIONS. Freed from years of struggle with the supporters of Ashland College after 1939, the Grace leaders could now use their considerable talents and enthusiasm in *missions, evangelism, and church growth. The division left them with about half of the Brethren membership and 70 congregations. A great deal of attention was focused on foreign missions. During the years of controversy (1936-39), most of the personnel and leadership of the Foreign Missionary Society supported the Grace viewpoint. Much of the support for the society came from congregations that favored Grace Seminary. From the time of the division until the present the Foreign Missionary Society has continued to expand its ministry. It now supports over one hundred missionaries in eight fields. The extent of this growth can be illustrated by the fact that the offering to the Foreign Missionary Society in the year of division (1939) was $50,818 whereas in 1981 it amounted to $1,984,196.

Although the foreign missionary cause occupied a central position in church life, the work of home missions was also important. Because of the struggles within the church, the Grace group had organized the Brethren Home Missions Council on Sept. 3, 1938, at Winona Lake. The leadership in this movement was provided by *R. Paul Miller. His evangelistic fervor was infused into the home mission program with dramatic results. The council has done a notable work in starting new congregations. The growth in numbers has come from reaching individuals from Brethren and non-Brethren backgrounds with the saving message of Christ. Not only have new congregations been established in the suburban areas of the USA, the council has also supported works among the Navajos, the Jews, the Hispanics, and the people of Kentucky.

An examination of the financial reports issued by the council shows that in the year 1940 the total income for the work of home missions was $25,244, whereas in the year 1981 it was $1,132,237. In 1940 twenty mission points were supported financially while in 1981 the number had increased to over fifty. In the forty-one years between these dates, dozens of church bodies have become self-supporting as a result of the aid of the council.

Another important organization that has aided in church growth is Grace Theological Seminary. Beginning in rented quarters, it expanded to include not only a graduate school of theology but also a liberal arts college on a spacious campus at Winona Lake. In 1982 ca. nine hundred students were enrolled in the college and nearly five hundred in the seminary. Most of the pastors serving Grace Brethren congregations in 1983 are graduates of Grace Schools.

Other cooperating organizations were founded to serve the same needs as those that remained in the hands of the Ashland group. These included a council for women's work, one for youth ministries, a publication company, a national ministerium, and a corporation to establish and manage a retirement home. Most of the affiliated organizations are operated from headquarters in Winona Lake.

BELIEF AND PRACTICES. Developments in the belief and practices of the FGBC which make it unique among the different groups of Brethren churches can be illustrated through a comparison of the "Message of the Brethren

Ministry" of 1921 with the "Statement of Faith of the National Fellowship of Brethren Churches" adopted by the Annual Conference in Aug., 1969. Although it was described as a revision of the earlier document there are significant differences between the two statements. The latter declaration is presented in a more scholastic form; its statements are supported by proof texts from the Scriptures and certain sections such as those dealing with the *Bible, the *church, the Christian life, and *eschatology are expanded. The more recent statement supports *baptism by trine immersion and the threefold *communion consisting of *feetwashing, the *Lord's supper, and partaking of the bread and the cup. Other distinctive Brethren practices are placed in the section on the Christian life, which is described as one of separation (*nonconformity) "from the evil ways of the world." The Christian should tell the truth, maintain the sanctity of the home, avoid litigation (*law) especially with other believers, not engage in carnal strife, maintain a prayer life, and practice the *anointing of the sick with oil. The church is defined as the company of all believers during the age of grace who meet in local autonomous groups for worship, edification, and witness.

The most notable divergence between the two documents is in the 1969 statement's elaborate eschatological section. The 1921 document with its general comments on the second coming is replaced with articles on Satan, the Second Coming, and the future life. The devil is described as a personal being who is doomed but, in the meantime, has the ability to oppose God's people. Christ's return is explained as visible, personal, and imminent. The second coming is to be in two stages; the first, to rapture, or remove, the church from earth before the tribulation period and, the second, to descend with the church to establish the thousand-year kingdom of God on earth. Details of the future life include the conscious existence of the dead, the *resurrection of the body, the reward of

believers with eternal life, and the condemnation of
unbelievers to eternal punishment. Throughout the document there is an obvious stress on the Bible as "verbally
inspired in all parts, and therefore wholly without error as
originally given by God."

It is clear that some Brethren distinctives found in the
earlier document are not given as much importance in the
later statement. According to the "Message of the
Brethren Ministry", believers "should 'be not conformed
to this world, but be transformed by the renewing of the
mind;' should not engage in carnal strife; and should
'swear not at all.'" As noted above, the 1969 document
subsumes some of these practices under the general
heading of the Christian life with such activities as prayer,
truthfulness, home life, and exhibiting the fruits of the
spirit. The duty of non-swearing is not even mentioned.

An explanation of the background for those changes
will help to characterize the outlook of the Grace
Brethren. The adoption of the statement of faith repre-
sents to a great extent the impact of Alva J. McClain on
the fellowship through his role as professor of theology at
Grace Seminary. He has often been described as a Calvinist, and to a certain extent this is true. However, if his
dispensational eschatology is taken into account, he
would be more accurately classed as a modified Calvinist.
His emphasis on the sovereignty of God, the eternal
security of the believer, and salvation by faith alone
would place him among Reformed theologians. He frequently reminded his students that God controlled every-
thing from the fall of a sparrow to the fall of an empire.
He was also less interested in strict adherence to church
practice than most of his Ashland colleagues. Typical of
many Grace Brethren he had studied in places where
dispensational fundamentalism was taught, such as Xenia
Theological Seminary. His works, including *Law and
Grace* and the *Greatness of the Kingdom*, presented a
form of dispensationalism which distinguished between

law and grace in such a way as to de-emphasize the role of ethical guidance in the life of the believer during the age of grace. He also taught that there is a universal kingdom of God which never ceases to exist which contrasts with the mediatorial kingdom. The latter kingdom was offered to the Jews at the time of Christ but they rejected it. Consequently Israel has been replaced by the church during the present age, but it will be restored to God's favor when Christ returns. McClains' views were accepted by many non-Brethren fundamentalists and he was made a member of the committee to revise the *Scofield Reference Bible*. Most of the ministers in the FGBC either studied under him or were influenced by him and preached dispensational theology from their pulpits. The major innovations in the 1969 statement result from the influence of McClain's theology. One aspect of his thought which was so universally held by Grace Brethren that it did not need to be mentioned was the eternal security of the believer.

As the Grace Brethren move closer to mainstream evangelical-fundamentalism, many of their distinctive beliefs seem less important. Although they still occasionally make statements opposing participation in carnal strife, nonparticipation in war is not stressed and the majority of young men serve in a regular combat position if they are confronted with *military service. The FGBC supports the military *chaplaincy as a missionary work and it has consistently produced its full quota of chaplains. The traditional Brethren emphasis in nonconformity to the world has been replaced by the separated life of the fundamentalists. In common with other groups this involves a series of restrictions that forbid smoking (*tobacco), drinking *alcoholic beverages, dancing, attending theaters, and similar *amusements. Church life is characterized by an emphasis on *evangelism and the preaching of Bible prophecy. Methods of church extension still depend upon the formulas worked out in the 1930s. A staunch stand against the ecumenical movement

and the *National Council of Churches of Christ is maintained.

Among the other conservative evangelical trends reflected in the attitudes of the FGBC are opposition to
*abortion, feminism, rights for homosexuals, *charis-
matics, and *evolution. A Sanctity of Life Committee was
appointed in 1981 to educate the churches concerning the
abortion problem. At the 1977 Annual Conference the
resolutions committee expressed the feelings of most
Grace Brethren when it equated abortion with murder
and condemned the Supreme Court decision of 1973
legalizing abortion as being in opposition to God's Word.
The same resolution included this statement supporting
punishment of those who commit murder: "The Bible
teaches that in order to preserve the sanctity of the human
life, and to insure the safety and dignity of all people, the
act of murder should be punished by the forfeiting of the
life of the murderer (Gen. 9:6; Lev. 24:17, 21). Therefore,
we resolve that capital punishment is a sacred responsibility given to government to be performed in all cases of
deliberate and premeditated murder. The various
Supreme Court decisions now in effect calling capital
punishment 'cruel and unusual punishment' are in opposition to the Word of God, and should be reversed to make
capital punishment mandatory in the cases of deliberate
and premeditated murder."

The Grace Brethren have also opposed the Equal
Rights Amendment and the struggle for women's liberation. They teach that the traditional *family with the
strong authoritarian father is the proper model for home
life. The wife "is to be in submission to her husband as she
would be to Christ (Eph. 5:22; Col. 3:18; I Peter 3:1;
Titus 2:4-5). She is to be a helper to him as he endeavors
to lead his family in godliness. The Equal Rights Amendment has brought . . . national crisis. We affirm the
equality of both men and women before God. We also affirm the functional order of home and church as stated in

the Scripture—Jesus Christ, man, woman (I Cor. 11:3). This order insures proper function in family, church and nation. It does not destroy the value or responsibility of women. It is God's established order of function and social relationships. We affirm that our standard of conduct is the Bible and not the current trend of society."

An earlier statement reinforced the church practice of not allowing women to be ordained elders: "the writers of Scripture did envision, among other things, *some* limitation on the teaching ministry of women in the church (I Tim. 2:11-15), a hierarchy of headship (I Cor. 11:3-16), limitations on eligibility for the eldership (I Tim. 3:2-5), the wife's responsibility to submit to her husband as unto the Lord (Eph. 5:22-24), and some sense in which the wife is the 'weaker vessel' thereby deserving special respect by the husband (I Peter 3:7)."

Members of the FGBC generally oppose the movement for rights of homosexuals and associate it with pornography and moral decay. The Conference of 1977 concluded "that homosexuality is in opposition to God's will for man and is a sinful act which demonstrates the depravity of the human soul outside of Christ (Lev. 18:22; 20:13; Rom. 1:26-27; I Cor. 6:9). Therefore, we are opposed to the current 'Gay Movement' and its demands for so-called 'equal rights for Gays.' We support those who are in opposition to this movement. We strongly oppose the current climate of pornography and sexual freedom that is evident by the multiplication of adult bookstores, X-rated movies, and the promiscuity that is evident in most television programming."

The *charismatic renewal of the 20th century also posed problems for the members of the Grace Brethren. Their biblical literalism and evangelistic activities have brought them into contact with many individuals who believe that divine healing is part of the atonement and that speaking in tongues is a necessary sign of the new birth. Several Grace congregations have divided over these matters. Consequently, resolutions have been passed at the Annual Conference encouraging pastors to preach about the Holy Spirit and to explain the weaknesses and "errors" of pentecostalism.

CREATIONISM AND INSPIRATION. Grace Brethren also reject the theory of evolution and teach what they call creationism in their schools and churches. The opposition to evolution, probably more than any other single factor, has led the churches to found Christian elementary and secondary schools. The FGBC will not compromise its stand on creation; the 1982 Annual Conference stated: "We believe that God's work of creation constitutes a unique testimony to His power and His regard for man (Isa. 40:12-31). Since no human being observed God's original work of creation, we are totally dependent upon God's revelation in Scripture for an understanding of how, in what sequence, and during what period of time God did this great work (Heb. 11:3). Therefore, we reaffirm our faith in the historical and scientific truth of the Genesis creation account and reject all compromising positions such as the theory of theistic evolution."

The Grace Brethren also believe in the "verbal, plenary inspiration of the Bible." They have supported that wing of the fundamentalist-evangelical movement that has found a spokesman in Harold Lindsell, who warned his readers that any group "that departs from belief in an inerrant Scripture will likewise depart from other fundamentals of the faith and at last cease to be evangelical in the historical meaning of the term."

The 1982 Annual Conference resolution explained the inspiration of the Bible in the following manner: "We believe that the 66 books of the Old and New Testaments are the complete and final revelation from God to man . . . We believe that 'inspiration' refers to the writings and not the writers, and that it guarantees the reliability, authenticity, accuracy, and authority of the original autographs (2 Tim. 3:16). We believe that the human authors of Holy

Scriptures were controlled by the Holy Spirit to the point that what they actually wrote down was kept absolutely free from any error, even though their writings reflect their individual styles and vocabularies (2 Peter 1:16-21) . . . We believe that the Bible is true and truth in that all that is written is accurately reported and that all it says actually occurred or will occur. It is the only objective basis for authority in the world because it is the direct revelation of the only true God (John 17:17)."

A new generation of leadership within the church faces a major problem that has developed from success in evangelism and church growth. It must struggle with the dilemma of what to do when non-Brethren people, who feel that they have been properly baptized and are content with their own observance of communion, wish to join a Grace Brethren church. Should they be required to be rebaptized and to observe the threefold communion? Some congregations believe that they should not be rebaptized and that Brethren churches should have a bread and cup communion in addition to the threefold service. Others disagree with this position. The debate over these matters has led to an attempt to arrive at a more comprehensive constitution and manual of procedure for the FGBC. Despite the fact that most pastors support such a move, a survey taken by moderator Luke E. Kauffman as reported in his address to the Annual Conference in 1982, indicated that about a third of the ministers were not comfortable with the attempt to achieve a greater degree of uniformity.

The FGBC appears to be the only Brethren group that is growing. It has developed impressively since the division of the 1930s. However, because of the addition of many individuals who do not understand or appreciate Brethren distinctions, it has become in many ways an example of an evangelical church which has more in common with fundamentalist Baptist, Presbyterian, or Independent Bible groups than with other branches of

Dunkers. A steady stream of young people attending such institutions as *BIOLA, Wheaton College, *Moody Bible Institute, Dallas Theological Seminary, and Bob Jones U. seems to indicate that the trend will continue. Yet Grace Brethren are forced to remain outside the mainstream of the fundamentalist movement because of their commitment to such ordinances as trine immersion baptism and the threefold communion service.

ADDITIONAL READING

Ankrum, Freeman, *Sidelights on Brethren History*. Elgin, IL: Brethren Press, 1962. 174p, illus.

Bittinger, Emmert F. *Heritage and Promise: Perspectives on the Church of the Brethren,* revised edition. Elgin, IL: Brethren Press, 1983. 158p, illus.

Brown, Dale W. *Understanding Pietism*. Grand Rapids, MI: Eerdmans, 1978. 182p.

Brumbaugh, Martin G. *History of the German Baptist Brethren in Europe and America*. Elgin, IL: Brethren Publishing House, 1899. xxii, 559p, illus. Reprinted 1907, 1961, and 1971.

Burkey, Fred and others. *The Brethren: Growth in Life and Thought* (Ashland, OH: Board of Christian Education, [1975]). iv, 202p.

Durnbaugh, Donald F. "The Brethren in Early American Church Life," in *Continental Pietism and Early American Christianity,* ed. F. Ernest Stoeffler. Grand Rapids, MI: Eerdmans, 1976). pp. 222-265.

Durnbaugh, Donald F., ed. *The Church of the Brethren: Past and Present*. Elgin, IL: Brethren Press, 1971. 182p.

Eller, David B. "The Brethren in the Western Ohio Valley, 1790-1850: German Baptist Settlement and Frontier Accomodation." Ph.D. dissertation, Miami University, 1976. 238p.

Ensign, C. David. "Radical German Pietism." Ph.D. dissertation, Boston University, 1955. 448p.

Holsinger, Henry R. *History of the Tunkers and the Brethren Church*. Lathrop, CA: author, 1901. 826p, illus. Reprinted 1962.

Kent, Sr., Homer A. *Conquering Frontiers: A History of the Brethren Church,* revised edition. Winona Lake, IN: Brethren Missionary Herald, 1972. 245p, illus.

Kimmel, John M. *Chronicles of the Brethren*. Covington, OH: Little Printing Co., 1951. 324p.

Lehman, James H. *The Old Brethren*. New York: Pillar Books, 1976. 384p, illus.

Mallott, Floyd E. *Studies in Brethren History*. Elgin, IL: Brethren Press, 1954. 382p, illus. Reprinted 1980.

Miller, Marcus. *"Roots by the River." The History, Doctine, and Practice of the Old German Baptist Brethren in Miami County, Ohio*. Piqua, OH: Hammer Graphics, Inc., 1973. 255p, illus.

Ronk, Albert T. *History of the Brethren Church*. Ashland, OH: Brethren Publishing Company, 1968. 524p, illus.

Sappington, Roger E. *Brethren Social Policy*. Elgin, IL: Brethren Press, 1961. 220p.

Schultz, Lawrence W. *Schwarzenau Yesterday and Today,* revised edition. Winona Lake, IN: author, 1977. 127p, illus.

Stoffer, Dale R. "The Background and Development of Thought and Practice in the German Baptist Brethren (Dunker) and the Brethren (Progressive) Churches (c. 1650-1979)." Ph. D. thesis, Fuller Theological Seminary, 1980, ix, 805p.

Willoughby, William G. *Counting the Cost*. Elgin, IL: Brethren Press, 1979.

Source Books

Durnbaugh, Donald F., ed. *European Origins of the Brethren*. Elgin, IL: Brethren Press, 1958. 463p, illus. First in a series.

Durnbaugh, Donald F., ed. *The Brethren in Colonial America*. Elgin, IL: Brethren Press, 1967. 659p, illus. Second in a series.

Sappington, Roger E., ed. *The Brethren in the New Nation*. Elgin, IL: Brethren Press, 1976. 496p, illus. Third in a series.

Hark, J. Max, trans. *Chronicon Ephratense: A History of the Community of Seventh Day Baptists at Ephrata, Lancaster County, Penna.* Lancaster, PA: S. H. Zahm, 1889. xvi, 288p. Reprinted 1972.

Miller, J. William, ed. *Christian Handbook and Rights and Ordinances*. Berne, IN: author, 1975. Varied pagination.

TOPICAL INDEX

Abortion, 110
Academies, 23, 24, 95
Acculturation, 24, 29, 33-34, 38-39, 69, 75, 76
Adjoining elders, 16
Affirmation, 17. *See also* Oathtaking.
AFSC, 82
Agriculture, 15, 20, 22, 24, 35, 39, 70, 80, 82, 83
Alcohol, use of, 82, 97, 109
Alternate service, 79-81
Amish, 14
Amusements, 109, 111. *See also* Recreation.
Anabaptism, Anabaptists, 9, 12, 46, 50, 84, 86
Annual meeting, 16-17, 18, 20, 22, 23, 26, 29-30.
   See also General conference, National conference
Annual meeting/conference (CB), 70, 71, 75-76, 79,
   80, 81, 86-87, 88, 90, 94, 96
Annual meeting (OGBB), 30, 32, 33, 34-35
Anointing, 31, 51, 99, 107. *See also* Healing
Antinomianism, 44-45
Appalachians, residents of, 88, 106
Architecture, 76-77. *See also* Meetinghouses.
Art, 13, 77.
Ashland Brethren. *See* Brethren Church
Ashland College, 43, 44-45, 46, 102-03
Ashland Theological Seminary, 43, 44-45, 46,
   102-03
Atonement, 47, 48, 97
Authority, 26, 32, 35, 37, 43, 86, 89, 98, 99, 102
Automobiles, use of, 34, 36, 37

Baptism, 10, 11, 13, 17, 31, 32, 45, 50-51, 70, 91,
   97, 99, 104, 107, 114
Beards, 33, 75
Beliefs. *See* Doctrines
Believer's baptism. *See* Baptism
Believers' Church, 89
Bethany Bible School. *See* Bethany Theological
   Seminary
Bethany (Brethren) Hospital, 90
Bethany Theological Seminary, 74, 85, 87, 90
Bible. *See* Scriptures
Bible prophecy, 98, 109
Bicentennial (1908), 70
Big meeting. *See* Annual meeting
Blacks, 82-83, 88
Blue Ridge College, 83
Bowman Brethren, 22
Brethren (1708-1883) 9-27
Brethren, expansion of, 10-12, 13, 14-15, 19-21
Brethren, formation of, 10-11
Brethren, migration of, 12-13, 14-15, 19-22
Brethren Action Movement, 81
Brethren Church, 26, 41-52, 69, 103-05, 106. *See
   also* Progressive Brethren
Brethren in Christ, 21
Brethren-Orthodox exchange, 87
Brethren Peace Fellowship, 81
Brethren Revival Fellowship, 86

Brethren Service Committee/Commission, 80
Brethren Volunteer Service, 80-81, 83
Bridgewater College, 73
Buggies (horse-drawn), 37
Business, 23-24. *See also* Economics

Calvinism, 108, 113. *See also* Reformed Church
Camping, 74-75, 90, 94
Capital punishment, 110
Celibacy, 13
Chaplaincy, military 109
Charismatic movement, 12, 32, 37-38, 88, 110,
   111-12
Christian Brethren, 21
Christian day schools, 35. *See also* Private schools
Christian education, 42, 43, 74, 77, 95, 101, 112
Christology, 31, 46-48, 51-52, 97, 107. *See also*
   Trinity
Christ's Assembly (Christi Menighed), 37-38
Chronicle. *See* Histories
Church, view of the, 9, 50, 89, 94, 107
Church extension, 42, 91, 109
Church growth, 21, 31, 38, 70, 91, 105, 113. *See
   also* Membership
Church of God (New Dunkers), 22
Church of God (Winebrennarian), 21
Church of North India, 72
Church of the Brethren, 43, 45, 69-91, 93-94. *See
   also* German Baptist Brethren
Church of the Brethren in Nigeria, 72
Church offices/officers, 15, 22, 76. *See also*
   Deacons, Elders. Ministers
Church-state relations, 10, 11, 17-18, 26-27, 78-83,
   110
Church structures, 89-90
Church visit. *See* Deacons' visit
Church World Service, 83-84
CIO, 82
Civil rights, 82
Civil War (American), 26-27
Civil War (Spanish), 79, 83
Civilian Public Service, 80
COCU, 86-87
Colleges, 23, 24, 35, 43, 44, 45, 73-74, 82, 83, 92,
   95, 102-03, 104, 105, 106
Collegiants (Dutch), 12
Colonization, 20, 31, 70
Communion, 31, 32, 46, 51, 77, 97, 99, 107, 113,
   114. *See also* Love feast
Communism. *See* Marxism
Community of True Inspiration, 38
Conciliar movement, 85, 87
Conditional security, 49. *See also* Eternal security
Confession, 31, 97
Confirmation, 51
Congregations, 20-21, 26, 29-30, 31, 32, 36, 38, 41,
   91, 99. *See also* Polity
Congregationalism, 16, 37, 43, 50, 76, 101, 103-04

Conscientious objection, 78-80. *See also* Nonresistance
Conscription, 17-18, 78-80. *See also* Military service
Consensus, 23, 50
Conservative Brethren, 69
Conversion, 20, 25, 49, 70, 101. *See also* Evangelism
Costume. *See* Dress, prescribed
Covenant, 9, 20, 50, 87
Creationism, 112
Creeds, 44, 47-48. *See also* Noncreedalism
CROP, 84

Deaconesses, 22
Deacons, 22, 33, 36, 50, 51, 95, 99
Deacons' visit, 32, 99
Delegates, 41-42, 100, 102
Devotional books, 73
Disaster relief, 43
Disciples of Christ, 21
Discipleship, 9-10, 42, 44
Discipline, 16, 17, 32, 37, 75, 98, 99, 101
Dispensationalism, 50, 108-09
Displaced persons, 83
Dissension, 12, 25. *See also* Division, Schism
Districts, 23, 25, 41, 70, 74, 75, 85, 90, 99, 101
District meetings, 41, 42, 99-100, 101
Division, 14, 23-27, 34, 36-38, 44-45, 69, 76, 85, 86, 88, 93-94, 102-05, 111-12. *See also* Dissension, Schism
Divorce, 94
Doctrines, 9, 12, 25, 31-32, 33, 46-52, 73, 97, 106-13
Double mode (feetwashing), 32
Dress, prescribed, 23, 32-33, 75-76, 94, 97-98
Dunkard Brethren, 76, 85, 93-100
Dunkards, 69
Dunkers, 69

Economics, 11, 12, 35, 71, 82, 84, 85, 91, 99, 106
Ecumenism, 17, 76, 79, 83-84, 85-87, 109-10
Editors, 23-25, 43, 71, 72
Education, 70, 73, 95, 112. *See also* Christian education, Higher education
Educational institutions, 24, 35. *See also* Academies, Colleges, Private schools, Theological seminaries
Ekklesiyar 'Yan'uawa a Nigeria, 72
Elders, 16, 22, 26, 30, 33, 50, 51, 87, 91, 95, 99, 100, 111
Election, divine, 32, 49. *See also* Eternal security
Election, political, 73, 82
Electricity, use of, 34, 37
Elizabethtown College, 73
Emigration, 12-13, 14-15
Ephrata Community, 13, 38
ERA, 110
Eschatology, 51-52, 107-09. *See also* Millennialism, Rapture
Espionage, 18
Established churches, 11, 88-89
Eternal security, 32, 45, 104, 108. *See also* Conditional security
Ethics, 44-45, 52
Eucharist, 51, 107, 113. *See also* Communion, Love feast
Evangelical Association, 21
Evangelism, 10-11, 13, 22, 25, 39, 43, 69, 70, 71, 86, 91, 101, 105, 109, 113

Evolution, 112

Faith, 31, 97, 108
Family, 20, 24, 34, 35, 110-11
Far Western Brethren, 22
Farming. *See* Agriculture
FAUS (SHARE), 88
Feetwashing, 31, 51, 97, 109. *See also* Double mode, Single mode
Fellowship of Grace Brethren Churches, 45, 86, 101-14
Feminism, 87, 110
Fraktur, 13
Freedom of religion, 11
Free ministry. *See* Ministry, unsalaried
Free Will Dunkers (Lemonites), 21
Fundamental Brethren Churches, 86
Fundamentalism, Fundamentalists, 44, 52, 85-86, 87, 101, 108, 109, 112, 114

Garb. *See* Dress, prescribed
General Conference (BC), 41-42, 43, 44, 45-46, 103
General Conference (DB), 76, 99-100
General Offices (CB), 89, 90
German Baptist Brethren, 26, 29-30, 69. *See also* Church of the Brethren
Glossolalia, 38, 111
"Goshen Statement", 78-79
Grace, 45, 47, 109
Grace Brethren. *See* Fellowship of Grace Brethren Churches
Grace College, 45, 102, 106
Grace Schools. *See* Grace College, Grace Theological Seminary
Grace Theological Seminary, 45, 102, 103, 105, 106, 108

Healing, 38, 111. *See also* Anointing
Heaven, 52, 107-08
Heifer Project, 79, 84
Hell, 52, 108
Higher education, 23, 24, 35, 43, 69, 84, 95, 114. *See also* Colleges, Theological seminaries
Hispanics, 88, 106
Historic Peace Churches, 79, 87, 89
Histories, 9, 13-14, 45, 73
Holiness, 47
Holy Kiss. *See* Kiss, holy
Holy Roman Empire (German Nation), 10
Holy Spirit, 48, 88, 96, 97
Homosexuality, 110, 111
Honites, 21
Human nature, 31, 47, 48, 97
Hymnals, 12, 15, 19, 69, 77
Hymns, 12, 77

ICYE, 84
Immersion. *See* Baptism
Incarnation, 48
Indians. *See* Native Americans
Infant baptism, 10
Insurance, 42, 98
Interchurch World Movement, 85
IVS, 84

Japanese-Americans, 82
Jewelry, 97-98
Jews, 50, 106
Juniata College, 24, 73, 85

Justification, 48-49

Kiss, holy, 31, 32, 33, 97
Korean War, 80-81

Labor unions, 82, 97
Land companies, 70
Landsites (Christian Brethren), 21
Language shift, 15, 69, 87
Lardin Gabas, 72
Law, divine, 109
Lawsuits, 98, 104-05, 107
Laying on of hands, 51
Leedy Brethren, 21
Legalism, 32, 44
Lemonites (Free Will Dunders), 21
Liberalism, 44, 85, 86, 102
Liturgy, 77-78
Lodges. See Secret societies
Lot, 10
Love, 47
Love feast, 13, 16, 31, 32, 46, 51, 77, 97. See also
    Communion, Eucharist
Loyalism (Toryism), 17, 18
Lutheran Church, 10, 14, 88-89

McPherson College, 73
Manchester College, 73, 82
Marriage, 31, 94, 99
Marxism, 72, 85
Mass media, 34, 97
Material aid, 83, 84
Medicine, 39, 80
Meetinghouses, 15-16, 33, 76-77
Membership, 14, 25, 31, 38, 41, 45, 50, 69, 70, 76,
    89, 91, 113
Mennonites, 9, 11, 14, 17, 79, 87, 89
Mental hospitals, 80
Miami Valley Brethren, 26, 30
Military service, 18, 78-81, 109. See also Conscien-
    tious objection
Millennialism, 22, 52, 107-08
Ministers, 33, 36, 42, 50, 95, 99, 101
Ministry, 15
Ministry, degrees of, 22
Ministry, salaried, 23, 42, 74, 77, 91, 95
Ministry, unsalaried, 15, 74
Minorities, 88, 106
Misión Mutua en las Américas, 72
Mission One, 88
Mission Twelve, 88
Mission Guidelines (CB), 72
Mission, Argentine, 42, 44, 45
Mission, Chinese, 71-72, 93
Mission, Columbian, 42
Mission, Danish, 25, 71
Mission, Ecuadorian, 71
Mission, Indian, 42, 71, 93
Mission, Malaysian, 42
Mission, Mexican, 42
Mission, Nigerian, 45, 71, 93
Mission, Oubangui-Chari, 44
Missions, education, 71
Missions, foreign, 23, 25, 42, 43-44, 45, 69, 71-72,
    93, 105
Missions, home, 23, 24, 44, 69, 70-71, 79, 91, 100,
    102, 105-06
Missions, urban, 71. See also Urban areas
Mobility, 35

Modernism, 44, 85, 86
Monasticism, 13
Monitor meetings, 96-97
Moravian Church, 17
Music, 13, 76, 78. See also Hymnals, Hymns,
    Musical instruments
Musical instruments, 77, 98
Mutuality (missions), 71

Names (church), 10, 26, 69-70
National Association of Evangelicals, 43
National Brethren Bible Conference, 103
National Conference (FGBB), 101-02, 112
National Council of Churches, 83-84, 85, 110
National Fellowship of Brethren Churches. See
    Fellowship of Grace Brethren Churches
Native Americans, 17, 88, 106
New Call to Peacemaking, 87
New Dunkers (Church of God), 22
New Testament. See Scriptures
New Windsor Center (BSC), 83-84
NISBCO, 80
Noncombatants, 78, 79
Nonconformity, 31, 32, 34, 51, 75, 94, 101, 107
Noncreedalism, 97
Nonregistration (draft), 81
Nonresistance, 17-18, 31, 51, 78, 97, 108. See also
    Conscientious objection
Nonswearing, 51. See also Oathtaking
Northern Baptist Theological Seminary, 87
NSBRO, 80

Oathtaking, 17, 32, 51, 98, 108
Obedience, 31, 44, 46, 49, 52, 98
Old Brethren, 36-37
Old Brethren German Baptists, 37
Old German Baptist Brethren, 26, 29-39, 69, 97
Old German Baptist Brethren of Greene Co., OH,
    37
Old Order, Old Orders, 26, 29-39, 69
Old Order German Baptist Brethren, 37
Old Testament. See Scriptures
On Earth Peace Assembly, 81
One Hundred Dunkers for Peace, 79
Ordinances, 19, 31, 51-52, 97
Ordination, 50, 51, 91, 99, 111
Ordination of women, 87
Orphanages, 90

Pacifism. See Nonresistance
Pastors. See Ministers, salaried
Peace, 79-80
Peace Corps, 84
Pennsylvania Synods, 17
Pentecost, 23, 33
Periodicals, 23-25, 29, 42, 72-73, 96
Persecution, 11-12, 18, 79
Petitions, 30
Pietism, 9, 10, 84
Politics, 27, 82, 85, 97. See also Church-state rela-
    tions; Election, political
Polity, 16-17, 22-23, 43, 50, 91, 98-100, 101, 103-04
Premillennialism, 51-52, 107-09. See also
    Eschatology
Printing. See Publishers, Publishing
Private schools, 35, 112. See also Christian educa-
    tion
Progressive Brethren, 26, 29, 34, 41, 43, 69, 101, 103
Prohibition, 73, 82

Protestantism, 9, 46, 70, 77, 85, 86-87. *See also* Lutheran Church, Reformed Church

Protracted meetings, 25, 70. *See also* Revivalism

Publication, Publications, 12, 18-19, 23-24, 34, 43, 71, 72-73, 74, 77, 93

Publishers, Publishing, 13, 18, 23-24, 42, 70, 106

Puidoux conferences, 88-89

Quakers. *See* Society of Friends

Queries, 16

Radical Pietism, 9, 12

Radio, use of, 34, 37

Railroads, 20, 23, 70

Rapture, 52, 107

Rebaptism, 10, 45, 50-51, 91, 97, 114

Reconciliation, 14, 22

Recreation, 74, 97, 109. *See also* Amusements

Redemption, 31, 46-47, 48, 97

Reform, 24-25. *See also* Progressive Brethren

Reformed Church, 9, 14, 88-89, 108

Refugees. *See* Displaced persons, *Volksdeutsche*

Relief, 42-43, 79, 82-83, 85

Regions, 90

Religious education, 20, 24. *See also* Christian education

Repentance, 31, 97

Restorationist movement, 21, 52

Resurrection, 48

Retirement homes, 42, 90, 102, 106

Revelation, 46, 112

Revival, Revivalism, 14, 21, 23, 25, 70

Revolutionary War (American), 17-18

Righteousness, 31, 49, 98

Rural areas, 15, 35, 38. *See also* Agriculture

Russian Orthodox Church, 87

Sabbatarianism, 13

Salaried ministry. *See* Ministry, salaried

Salvation, 31, 44, 45, 48-49, 50

Sanctification, 49, 98

Satan, 107

Scriptures (Old Testament / New Testament), 9, 19, 31, 46-47, 48, 50, 74, 84, 97, 98, 104, 107, 108, 111, 112-13

Schism, 13, 21-22, 26-27, 29-31, 32, 36-38, 44-45, 76, 93-94, 102-05. *See also* Dissension, Division

Secret societies, 94, 97

Selective service, 79-80

Self-examination service, 32

Separatism, 11, 12

Sermons, 22, 23, 25, 77, 87, 99

SERRV, 84

Settlement, 12-15, 19-20, 70

SHARE. *See* FAUS

Shoemakerites (Brethren in Christ), 21

"Short and Sincere Declaration," 17

Simple life style, 23, 35, 36, 86, 98

Sin, 32, 46, 47, 48, 49, 51, 79, 97

Single mode (feetwashing), 51

Sino-Japanese War, 83

Slavery, 15, 27

Social gospel, 44, 85

Society, 17, 29, 33-34, 75, 111. *See also* Acculturation

Society of Friends (Quakers), 12, 16, 23, 79, 87, 89

Solingen Brethren, 11

Spanish Civil War. *See* Civil War (Spanish)

Spirituality, 88, 97, 108

Standing Committee, 23, 36, 99

Student exchanges, 83

Student Volunteer Movement, 71

Substitutes (military), 18, 78

Suburban areas, 38, 106

Sunday school curriculum, 42, 74, 86

Sunday schools, 23, 25, 41, 69, 74, 93

Tax refusal, 18, 78

Taxes, 18, 78

Technology, 24, 34, 39

Telephone, use of, 34, 36, 37

Television, use of, 34, 97, 111

Temperance, 82

Theological seminaries, 43, 44-45, 46, 74, 84, 87, 90, 102-03, 105, 106, 108

Theological study conferences (CB), 89

Theology, 46-52, 84-86, 89. *See also* Doctrines

Thurmanites, 22

Tobacco, use of, 97, 109

Tongues. *See* Glossolalia

Tracts, 73

Travel, 16, 22, 31, 34, 35. *See also* Colonization, Emigration, Mobility, Railroads, Settlement

Treason (Sedition), 18, 79

Trinity, 46, 47, 50, 97. *See also* Christology, Holy Spirit

United Evangelical Church of Ecudor, 72

United Nations, 82

Unity, 24, 32, 34, 36, 72, 76, 89

Universalism, 19, 21, 52

University of La Verne, 73

Urban areas, 15, 38

Vacation Bible schools, 74

Vietnamese War, 80-81

Volksdeutsche, 83

Voting, manner of, 23

War Between the States. *See* Civil War (American)

Westward movement, 19-22

Womaen's caucus (CB), 87

Women, 11, 42, 45, 50, 75, 87, 97, 98, 101, 102, 106, 110-11

Women in ministry, 22, 50, 87

Word. *See* Christology, Scriptures

Work camps, 83

Works, 31

World Council of Churches, 85

World War I, 78-79

World War II, 79-80

Worldliness, 24, 25, 75, 94, 101, 105. *See also* Acculturation

Worship, 15, 20-21, 41, 74, 77-78

Youth, 42, 71, 74-75, 81, 94-95, 101, 102, 106